MW01243788

# The Picture of Redemption in the Feasts of Israel

**Dr. G. Michael Saunders, Sr.**

*Therefore do not let anyone judge you by what you eat or drink, or with regard to a religious festival, a New Moon celebration or a Sabbath day. These are a shadow of the things that were to come; the reality, however, is found in Christ. (Colossians 2:16,17).*

This book is dedicated to the Bible Boys at the Holy Land Experience 2006-2008. They introduced me to joys of Biblical study for the purpose of finding the meanings - past, present and future - of the events in Scripture. Working with these men were some of the happiest days of my ministerial career. Thanks for everything brothers!

Dr. Bill Jones
Dr. George Fredericks
Dr. Herb Samworth

## The Jews

The Jewish religion affirms that life is here and now. At the same time, Jewish tradition insists that the final goal of paradise regained is equally worthy of our loyalty and effort. Judaism is the Jewish way to get humanity from the world as it is now to the world of final perfection. To get from here to there, you need both the goal and a process to keep you going over the long haul of history. In Judaism, the holidays supply both.

In the face of widespread evil and suffering, the holy days teach the central idea of redemption. They keep the idea real by registering the great events of Jewish history that validate the hope. In their variety, the holidays incorporate rich living experiences that sustain the human capacity to hold a steadfast course. Sacred days give sustenance to spiritual life and a dimension of depth to physical life. The holy days provide a record of the struggle to the covenant. While chronicling the history, they distill the lessons learned along the way. And because they are popular, the holidays make the dream and process of realization the possession of the entire people. (Irving Greenberg. *The Jewish Way* . p. 24.)

## The Christians

The Seven Feasts of Israel are first listed in their entirety in Leviticus 23 even though they are referenced in other Pentateuch books as well. Leviticus 23, however, is sometimes referred to as "God's calendar of redeeming grace" or the "calendar of divine redemption". These 44 verses basically tell of God's redemptive plan for the world He created as told through the Feasts of Israel. The holidays and Sabbath days are a "shadow of things to come" (Colossians. 2:16,17). (RW Research, Inc. *Feast and Holidays of the Bible*; Rose Publishing.)

# Table of Contents

# Preface

*The LORD said to Moses, "Speak to the Israelites and say to them: 'These are my appointed feasts, the appointed feasts of the LORD, which you are to proclaim as sacred assemblies. - Leviticus 23:1,2*

The more I study the Scriptures the more I become aware that the Bible only has one story and that is the story of Redemption. In Gen. 3:15 God promises to save us through the "seed of the woman" that we know is the Messiah. Once God makes that promise, everything He does points to that Messiah in some way and to the day that He will come and save us. What's more, almost everything God commands or instructs His people to do and live and believe point to the Messiah in some way.

The Feasts of Israel were given to God's people at Mt. Sinai when they had come out of Egypt and were receiving the moral law of God. These feasts had practical meaning for the people but not at the time they were given. You see the seven feasts of Israel could not be practiced while the people were wandering in the desert or while they were conquering the land. It was not until they were established in the land that the feasts could be fully observed. So when God gives them to the people, He is essentially saying, "The day will come when you will be able to observe these feasts and I want you to do them in this manner." In other words He gave them instructions about spiritual observances that that they were going to do in the future.

Now when the day came that the people could observes these feasts, they turned out to be very practical. The Lord knew that this would be an agricultural society and so He arranged the feasts and assigned their meanings to be concerned with this kind of life. The spring festivals have to do with planting and sowing and the promise of life and the fall festivals have to do with harvest and reaping and the thanksgiving for life's provisions. However these agricultural meanings were only the surface meanings. There were also deeper, spiritual meanings that that the Lord assigned to these festivals and He revealed these meanings to the people. So as they are celebrating the planting and the harvesting, they are also worshipping God with thanksgiving and praise and acknowledging that all they have has come from His loving hand. He is their provider and they rejoice in Him – specifically and nationally at the festival times.

Additionally, the Lord gave all the feasts a prophetic meaning. These feasts would all, in different ways, point to the coming Messiah who would be our ultimate provider of eternal life. So as we celebrate the life we have today and thank God for meeting our needs, we are to be looking forward to the day when we will celebrate eternal life with the one who has provided our salvation.

In Leviticus 23:6 is a Hebrew word translated as "feast." *"And on the fifteenth day of the same month is the feast (chag) of Unleavened Bread..."* The Hebrew word 'chag', which means a "festival", is derived from the Hebrew root word 'chagag', which means to move in a circle, to march in a sacred procession, to celebrate, dance, to hold a solemn feast or holiday. God gave the festivals as cycles to be observed yearly so that, by doing them, we can understand God's redemptive plan for the world, the role that the Messiah would play in that redemption, and our personal relationship to God concerning how we grow from a novice Bible believer to a mature Bible believer.

So the feasts of Israel, were practical, were relevant to life today, were God centered and worshipful and were also prophetic – pointing to the coming Messiah, salvation and eternal life. Lets look now at what the feasts teach us today and how we can use them in the worship of our Lord Jesus Christ and to grow in grace and in our faith and Christian experience.

Paul said in Colossians 2:16-17 that the Jewish feasts and celebrations were a shadow of the things to come through Jesus Christ . And though as Christians we may not commemorate these holidays in the traditional biblical sense, as we discover the significance of each, we will certainly gain a greater knowledge of God's Word, an improved understanding of the Bible, and a deeper relationship with the Lord.

## Chapter One - The Actual Circle Of Life

*We do have such a high priest, who sat down at the right hand of the throne of the Majesty in heaven, 2 and who serves in the sanctuary, the true tabernacle set up by the Lord, not by a mere human being. (Hebrews 8:1,2)*

What is the big picture of your life? Where is your life going? What is your life going to accomplish? Everyone has something going on in their life - good or bad. What is the big picture of our life? Who or what determines what the big picture of our life is?

It is important to remember that there actually is a big picture for your life. And interestingly, for Christians, it is the same big picture for everyone of us no matter what our lives are like. It is a big picture designed by God and really, it is a very simple big picture. In order to see this big picture I want to show you that...

### Our Lives Have A Direction - We Are Going Back Home!

### The Heavenly Sanctuary

In Hebrews 8:5 we are told that there is a Heavenly Sanctuary. *"They serve at a sanctuary that is a copy and shadow of what is in heaven. This is why Moses was warned when he was about to build the tabernacle: 'See to it that you make everything according to the pattern shown you on the mountain.'"* The author of Hebrews however, is quoting the words of God from the book of Exodus. When Moses was on the mountain talking with God, the Lord gave him all kinds of instructions and one of them was to build the Wilderness Tabernacle. However God says to Moses in verse 25:8 *"Then have them make a sanctuary for me, and I will dwell among them. Make this tabernacle and all its furnishings exactly like the pattern I will show you.*

When Moses actually gets ready to build the Tabernacle God reminds him again, *" See that you make them according to the pattern shown you on the mountain"* (Exodus 25:40). This even applied to the furnishings in the Tabernacle. Numbers 8:4 says, *"This is how the lampstand was made: It was made of hammered gold—from its base to its blossoms. The lampstand was made exactly like the pattern the LORD had shown Moses."*

We are again reminded of this sanctuary in the book of Acts in the speech of Stephen at his martyrdom when he says on Acts 7:44, *"Our ancestors had the tabernacle of the covenant law with them in the wilderness. It had been made as God directed Moses, according to the pattern he had seen."* So Hebrews 8 is telling us that there is a Heavenly Sanctuary and that the

Tabernacle was to be an illustration of that Heavenly Sanctuary to all God's people. The Presence, the Glory, and the Holy Spirit of God dwelt in that Heavenly Sanctuary.

### The Garden of Eden

God created man to *"glorify God and enjoy Him forever"* (1). God is so awesome, wonderful and glorious that He decided to create humans so that they could enjoy Him and enjoy His love and grace for them. In other words, God created us to find pleasure and happiness in Him, in loving Him and in His mighty creative works. Part of this pleasure was to be in the actual, physical presence of God and to see His glory and be filled with His Holy Spirit. Genesis 1:27-30 tells us that when God made man He touched Him and talked to Him and gave him instructions. Genesis 2 tells us the same thing. Genesis 3:8 tells us that God came to see Adam and Eve in the cool of the day - the best part of the day. So God is having a personal, face to face relationship with Adam and Eve in the perfect, sinless creation that He had made.

Then Adam and Eve brought sin into the world at the temptation of Satan (Genesis 3). Sin ruined man's relationship with God because sin cannot come into the presence of a Holy God. Sin in us keeps us from being in the presence of God. Our relationship with God is destroyed. Not broken or damaged but destroyed. We have lost our Father, we have lost our home. We are runaways living on the streets with no desire or ability to return to our home.

But God our Father will not let us go. He will not abandon us. He did not and will not cease to love us, just because we ceased to love Him. So God made a promise to fix the problem of our separation from Him through a Messiah that He would send (Genesis 3:15). From this point on, everything God does, everything that is recorded in the Scriptures, is about the Messiah, points to the Messiah and reveals the Messiah so that we will know Him when He comes and be ready to follow Him back to our real home.

### The Wilderness Tabernacle

We do not see the presence, glory or Spirit of God mentioned in the Scriptures again until we get to Mt. Sinai. We can see God's presence, glory and Spirit in all His actions but it is not recorded for us as it is in the Garden of Eden. But at Mt. Sinai we see that God is forming the Hebrew slaves, newly freed from Egypt, into the nation of Israel and the nation of His own people. Part of making them His people includes God's desire to dwell among His people. Because of sin He cannot. However, He devises a temporary solution to the problem that will become a permanent solution when the Messiah arrives. That temporary solution is the Wilderness Tabernacle that we see in Exodus

4

25:9. This Tabernacle is a dwelling place - where God meets with His people is a tent of meeting that is divided into two parts. One part for the people and one part for God separated by a veil that prevents sin from coming before God.

Here God can meet with His people personally. He can remind them of His love and His promise of salvation. And He can forgive their sins in a visual way. However, it is not face to face. It is through priests and sacrifices. And again it is only a partial and temporary solution.

Exodus 25:9 tells us about the building of the Tabernacle where Moses is reminded to build it according to the plans God showed him. Plans of the Heavenly Sanctuary that the Tabernacle is to be a model. Exodus 40:34,35 tells us about the dedication ceremony of the Tabernacle and we are told at last about the Presence, Glory and Spirit of God and how the *Presence, Glory and Spirit of God filled the Tabernacle* so fully that the priests could not go inside to do their ministry until the next day.

### Solomon's Temple

The Tabernacle lasted for 400 years and then God gave Solomon permission to build the first Temple. He tells Solomon not to change any details as they all point to the Messiah and to the Heavenly Sanctuary. So everything is the same but made with permanent materials.

Once again we are told in I Kings 8:10,11 about the dedication ceremony of Solomon's Temple which will now be God's dwelling place on the earth. The place where God will meet with His people. We are told once again that *the Presence, Glory and Spirit of God filled the Temple* so fully that the priests could not go inside to do their ministry until the next day.

### Zerubbabel's Temple

Solomon's Temple lasted 400 years and then it was destroyed by the Babylonians. After the return to Israel the Temple was rebuilt by Ezra and Nehemiah and under Governor Zerubbabel. In Haggai 2 we are told about the dedication of second temple. Here we are told that one day the Desire of Nations will come and when He does, God's *Presence, Glory and Spirit of God will be full in Him.*

### Herod's Temple

Herod's Temple is what we have labeled the Temple of the New Testament times. This Temple was not a new Temple but rather was the same one Zerubbabel had built. However, King Herod magnificently remodeled it and expanded the Temple Mount platform until the Temple and all her courts were the most beautiful buildings of the ancient world. What is interesting is that we are never told in Scripture how the Lord God felt about this remodel. We are not told that God was displeased over this remodel but He just never comments about it at all in Scripture. This is an interesting oddity since so much is said about the previous places of worship.

### The Lord Jesus Our Savior

We were told in Haggai 2 that the Presence and Spirit and Glory of God would be in the Temple until the Messiah came and then the Presence, Glory and Spirit of the Lord would go into the Messiah. So we know that from the time Zerubbabel built the Temple until the birth of Jesus the Lord God dwelt in the Temple. But when Jesus was born the Presence, Glory and Spirit of the Lord moved and dwelt in Jesus. We see this in Jesus at His baptism in in Luke 3:21,22 *"When all the people were being baptized, Jesus was baptized too. And as he was praying, heaven was opened and the Holy Spirit descended on him in bodily form like a dove. And a voice came from heaven: "You are my Son, whom I love; with you I am well pleased."* . Essentially Jesus is the living Temple of God. It is through Jesus that God lived among His people. It is through Jesus that the promised salvation comes to us. It is through Jesus that we can go home and return to our Father. It is through Jesus that we can once again have a face to face relationship with our Heavenly Father.

Jesus lived a sinless life on the earth. He fulfilled His mission perfectly. He died on the cross for us and the very moment He died on the cross, the Veil in the Temple, separating us from the physical, face to face presence of God was torn in two. God kept the promise He made to us in Genesis 3:15 and solved our sin problem. When Jesus said "It is finished" He was telling us that everything necessary for salvation had been accomplished. He had made it possible for us to come directly into the presence of our Holy God once again! Then He was buried. And on the third day He arose from the grave and salvation was finalized and accomplished!

Then, after completing His saving work, He returned to Heaven where He sits at the right hand of God the Father Almighty reining and ruling over us and all creation! One day He will return for us on the clouds of glory and we can't wait for that day. However, until He returns where is the Temple today? Where is the place on earth today where the Presence, the Spirit and Glory of God dwells among men?

### The Living Temple of God Today

Paul is the one who gives us the answer to this question. In I Corinthians 3:16 Paul tells us *"Don't you know that you yourselves are God's temple and that God's Spirit dwells in your midst? If anyone destroys God's temple, God will destroy that person; for God's temple is sacred, and you together are that temple."* Those of us who know Jesus Christ as our own personal Lord and Savior are the sanctuary of God, the Temple, the dwelling place of God on earth today. God our Father lives in our hearts and dwells among His people in us today. And it is through our words and lives that people of our world can find the message of saving faith through Christ. The Presence, Glory and Spirit of God fills us and lives in us!

### Returning Home

Hebrews 10:19-23 tells us *" Therefore, brothers and sisters, since we have confidence to enter the Most Holy Place by the blood of Jesus, by a new and living way opened for us through the curtain, that is, his body, and since we have a great priest over the house of God, let us draw near to God with a sincere heart and with the full assurance that faith brings, having our hearts sprinkled to cleanse us from a guilty conscience and having our bodies washed with pure water. Let us hold unswervingly to the hope we profess, for he who promised is faithful."* We are going to one day, go into the Holy Place and be able to draw near to our Father God.

When Jesus returns, the Presence, Glory and Spirit of God that is in us will be reunited with the Presence, Glory and Spirit that is in Jesus and we will all be together with our Father God just like we were in the Garden of Eden, at the first of creation, before sin came into the world. We will be with our family, our older brother Jesus and our Father God and we will be back in our home in the Heavenly Sanctuary, in the New Heavens and the New Earth, in the New Jerusalem, in the perfect creation, for all eternity

We are also told that Creation will receive its redemption too. Ephesians 1:8-10 says *" With all wisdom and understanding, he made known to us the mystery of his will according to his good pleasure, which he purposed in Christ, to be put into effect when the times reach their fulfillment—to bring unity to all things in heaven and on earth under Christ."* Just like us, all of creation is going somewhere rather than nowhere. Time itself is progressing toward a "fulfillment." God *"brings all things in heaven and on earth together under one head, even Christ."*

I illustrate this circle of life with the horrors of the earthquake of Haiti several years ago. In that earthquake there was a little girl that was rescued. She had lived in an orphanage and was in the process of being adopted by an American couple just before the quake. When the earthquake struck, the adoptive parents in the states lost track of the little girl. Now I suppose they could have said "Well, we will wait till the crisis is over and then we will either find her or adopt a different child." But this was impossible for them to say. You see they had already been to Haiti. They had been to the orphanage. They had already met the little girl. They had spent time with her. They had fallen in love with her. In their hearts she already was their daughter.

And like any loving parent would do, they jumped on an airplane and with great difficulty of travel, cost, politics, red tape and physical danger they got into Haiti and found their daughter. And when they found her lying under a tent on a dirty blanket she recognized them instantly and threw her arms around their necks and the couple told her with tears and laughter and joy, "Mommy and daddy are here."

Then they brought her home. She was born in Haiti. She is a Haitian girl by race. Yet her real home is in the arms of those who loved her and were willing to give their lives for her. Her real home is wherever they are.

So it is with Jesus. We are born of this world. We are of the sinful, broken human race. We live in the earthquake destruction of sin and evil every moment of every day. But this is not our home. Our home is in the arms of the One who loved us and who did, in fact, give His life for us. Our real home is wherever Jesus is. The big picture for Christians on earth is our journey back home and into His loving arms.

The Christian life then is our journey from sin to salvation, from brokenness to wholeness, from orphanage to home. All that we do, all the struggles and trials and tribulations, all the joys and victories and pleasures, all the sacrifices and growing pains and spiritual improvements, everything that we do and experience in this life as Christians are all part of our journey home. We live the Christian life as faithfully as we can in order to progress on our journey home. The significance and meaning of the Christian life is about going home. The purpose and goal of the Christian life is about going home. And the way we get home - *is by following the path that the Holy Spirit lays before us.* That path leads to Jesus whom we love and that is where home is. Life is hard in this world but we can have joy in our hearts even in the midst of crisis or trial or turmoil because every moment of every day we know that we are going home.

## *Only One Story*

In actuality the Bible only has one story which is Redemption - coming back home to God our Father through Jesus! God's plan for us is for us to be with Him again in paradise forever. He wants to give us redemption. He wants to give us His unconditional love, His total forgiveness of all our sins and His overwhelming grace. These gifts are available to us today - just by knowing Jesus Christ as our Savior and these are the gifts that will bring us home to our Father. Everything in Scripture, everything in the Christian faith, everything in life is all about the Lord Jesus Christ and is all about Him bringing us home to paradise.

My grandfather died in 2009 and we sang this chorus at his funeral:
*When Jesus Breaks the morning*
*The Host of Heaven will sing*
*Hosanna in the highest*
*It is our conquering King*

*We'll clasp our hands together*
*Around the great white throne*
*And join the Angels singing*
*At last! At last we're home!*

The purpose and goal of the Christian life is to go home and to be with Jesus in the restored and redeemed creation forever! All Christians, all who know Jesus Christ as their own personal Lord, are on this wonderful journey.

## Chapter Two – Salvation
## Pesach - Feast of Passover (Nisan 14)

*"...a night of solemn observance to the Lord for bringing them out of the land of Egypt" (Exodus 12:42).*

*This is how you are to eat it: with your cloak tucked into your belt, your sandals on your feet and your staff in your hand. Eat it in haste; it is the LORD's* **Passover** *(Exodus 12:10). The LORD's* **Passover** *begins at twilight on the fourteenth day of the first month (Leviticus 23:4). They must not leave any of it till morning or break any of its bones. When they celebrate the* **Passover** *, they must follow all the regulations (Numbers 9:11).*

*And Pharaoh rose up in the night, he and all his servants and all the Egyptians and there was a great cry in Egypt: And he called for Moses and Aaron at night and said: Rise up and get you forth from among my people, both ye and the children of Israel; and go serve the LORD as you have said...And the people took their dough before it was leavened, their kneading troughs being bound up in their clothes upon their shoulders (Exodus. 12:30-31, 34).*

The Seven Feasts of Israel are first listed in their entirety in Leviticus 23 even though they are referenced in other Pentateuch books as well. Leviticus 23, however, is sometimes referred to as "God's calendar of redeeming grace" or the "calendar of divine redemption". These 44 verses basically tell of God's redemptive plan for the world He created through the Feasts of Israel. The holidays and Sabbath days are a "shadow of things to come" (Colossians 2:16,17) (1).

For the Israelites living in Biblical times, the holidays were concentrated in two months: the first month of the year, Nisan, incorporated Passover, Unleavened Bread and First Fruits; and the seventh month Tishri incorporated the Feast of Trumpets, the Day of Atonement and the Feast of Booths. Nisan celebrates the beginning of salvation of the people and Tishri celebrates the beginning of the Nation of Israel. So Nisan is the Spiritual New Year and Tishri is the Civil New Year. However, both months were dominated by the Exodus holidays.

The only other holiday was Pentecost, which occurred in the third month. Passover, marking the liberation, and Booths, commemorating the journey, are the alpine events in the Hebrew Calendar. Pentecost is the link between the two major Exodus commemorations, marking the transformation of Exodus from a one-time event into an ongoing commitment (2).

### When is the Feast of Passover?

Now Passover is the oldest feast or holiday that has been continuously celebrated in the world. It has been celebrated for over 3500 years. It was given to the people for them to remember the deliverance of the people from Egypt and slavery and God's judgment. The month of the Passover is Nisan (called Abib before the Babylonian captivity – Exodus 13:4; 34:18 (3)) and this month became the first month of the Jewish Spiritual New Year from that time on (Exodus 12:2; Numbers 9:5; 28:16) (4).

The month of Nisan, is the equivalent of the second half of March/first half of April on our solar calendar (5). The Lord decreed that Passover was to be celebrated at sundown on the 14th of Nissan (Lev. 23:5) however, this date moves because the whole lunar calendar moves annually so it is not the same day of the year, every year, on the solar calendar.

In this week set aside by God, we are actually celebrating, three distinct holidays: the Feast of Passover, the Feast of Unleavened Bread, and the Feast of First Fruits. All of these occur on consecutive days. They are frequently all lumped together under the title "Passover Week" and are used interchangeably in Scripture, but they are three separate celebrations according to God's decree and so we will cover them in separate chapters.

### What Is the Feast of Passover?

The Exodus is the core event in Jewish history and religion. In Judaism's teachings, the Exodus is not a one-time event but a norm by which all of life should be judged and guided. The Exodus is an "orienting event" – an event that sets in motion and guides the Jewish way toward the Promised Land – an earth set free and perfected. The Exodus is brought into life and incorporated into national values through the classic Jewish behavior model – reenactment of the event. The basic rhythm of the year is set through the reenactment of the Exodus (Passover), followed by the acceptance of the Covenant (Pentecost), and then by re-staging the Exodus way (Feast of Tabernacles).

Judaism does look forward to a great future event, however. This event is the messianic redemption that will dwarf the importance of the Exodus. The Jewish people believe this event is yet to come. Christians know it has already occurred in Jesus the Christ, the Messiah.

The death, burial and resurrection of Jesus Christ are the core events in Christian history and religion. In Leviticus 23:2 it is written, "...the feasts of the Lord, which ye shall proclaim to be holy convocations..." The Hebrew term translated as convocation in Leviticus 23:2,4 is 'miqra', which means "a rehearsal". God gave the Festivals to be yearly "rehearsals" of the future events in the redemption. Because God gave the "rehearsals" to teach us about the major events in the redemption, if we want to understand those events, then we need to understand what God was teaching us by these rehearsals. Both the Exodus and Redemption are taught in the feasts. Both the deliverance from slavery in Egypt and the deliverance from sin, death and hell are represented **(6)**.

Passover itself is an event that only happened once in history. It was deliverance from the last and most costly of the 10 plagues that God sent on Egypt in order to get them to release the Hebrews from slavery. The Passover celebrations each year are memorials and reminders to the actual events of that terrible day. These annual celebrations point to the salvation and deliverance that God gave His people from the Egyptians. They also point to a future salvation and deliverance from eternal death through the Messiah. We read about Passover in Exodus 12, which says in part:

*1 Now the LORD said to Moses and Aaron in the land of Egypt, 2 "This month shall be the beginning of months for you; it is to be the first month of the year to you. 3 "Speak to all the congregation of Israel, saying, 'On the tenth of this month they are each one to take a lamb for themselves, according to their fathers' households, a lamb for each household... 6 'You shall keep it until the fourteenth day of the same month, then the whole assembly of the congregation of Israel is to kill it at twilight.*

*7 'Moreover, they shall take some of the blood and put it on the two doorposts and on the lintel of the houses in which they eat it... 11 'Now you shall eat it in this manner: with your loins girded, your sandals on your feet, and your staff in your hand; and you shall eat it in haste--it is the LORD'S Passover.*

*12 'For I will go through the land of Egypt on that night, and will strike down all the firstborn in the land of Egypt, both man and beast; and against all the gods of Egypt I will execute judgments--I am the LORD.*

*13 'the blood shall be a sign for you on the houses where you live; and when I see the blood I will pass over you, and no plague will befall you to destroy you when I strike the land of Egypt.*

The Lord struck the homes all those who did not have the blood of the lamb on the doorposts and lintels of their homes with the death of a child. This was the plague that broke Pharaoh's resolve to rebel against the Lord. Interestingly though, it was not enough to stop him from trying to get them back. But once again he met with disastrous tragedy when he took his army into the desert to try and stop them. Because of this momentous, divine event, God instituted Passover as "a night of solemn observance to the Lord for bringing them out of the land of Egypt" (Exodus 12:42). God commanded that Passover be observed as a memorial forever (Exodus 12:14).

### What is the Meaning of the Feast of Passover?

Passover is ultimately about salvation and the sacrifice needed for salvation. The original Passover was about salvation form Egypt and the lamb was the sacrifice needed. But there was a deeper meaning that the people themselves did not understand until much later. Even though the people were saved from Egypt, they were still under the judgment of God and without a sacrifice God's wrath would come on them eternally. The Passover memorials reminded the people that the blood of the lamb must also be applied to their hearts if they were to escape God's eternal judgment and wrath.

In the Passover memorial celebrations the people were to select a lamb without blemish that is without flaw or defect. It was to be taken out of the flock on the 10th day and then they were to keep the lamb for 4 days in their own homes. This allowed the family to observe the lamb and confirm that it was without blemish. It also allowed each family to become attached to the lamb so that it was no longer just a lamb, but it was *their* lamb and would impress upon them the costly nature of the sacrifice. An innocent one had to die in their place (Exodus 12:1-6).

After four days all the people brought the lambs to the temple and they were all present together as all the lambs were slaughtered. At the same time however, each family had to claim the effect of the sacrifice individually. At the original Passover this was seen in the fact that each family put the blood of their own lamb on their doorposts. In all the following memorials of Passover this was to be applied to their hearts. At that moment the innocent lamb became their substitute making it possible for the judgment of God to pass over them.

### How was the Feast of Passover to be celebrated?

According to the Exodus 12:3-13 and Leviticus 23:4-8, the Passover was to be celebrated by taking an unblemished, male, one year old lamb (from either sheep or goats) on the 10th of Nisan (the first month of the spiritual new year) and keeping it for four days. In the evening (twilight) of the 4th day (14th of Nisan) they were to kill it. Then they were to roast the entire lamb (head, entrails, everything) with fire and eat it with unleavened bread and bitter herbs. Anything left over was to be burned in the fire and not eaten the next day.

They were to eat the meal fully dressed, with their shoes on and their staff in their hand. This was because the Lord told them they were going to have to move quickly when the time came to leave Egypt. The Lord knew that after the passing over of death the Egyptians would be glad to see them go, but would then hate the Hebrews for the loss of their children and come after them. So everything had to be done fast, quick & easy - all preparations were to be made in advance.

The Passover meal became known as the Seder (SAY-der), which means, "order". God also decreed that the Passover should be celebrated with a rite (ritual) or service (Exodus12:25). The service has become known as the Haggadah (Ha-gaa–dah). In addition to the special foods that were eaten the service was to raise questions in the minds of the children so that the Exodus story could be rehearsed from generation to generation (Exodus 12:26-27).

Several centuries before Christ the service connected to the Passover became traditionalized. It had certain basic Scriptures that were to be read, songs that were to be song, prayers that were to be said and additional symbolic foods. Even though more songs and traditions were introduced to the Passover during the Middle Ages the Passover Seder remains almost the same as it was 2000 years ago (7).

### How was the Feast of Passover celebrated in Jesus' day?

It is important for us to know how Jesus spent Holy Week because when we look at Jesus fulfilling the Passover we want to understand everything that he fulfilled. The more I study the life of the Lord the more I come to understand that Jesus left no stone unturned. What I mean is that Jesus fulfilled *everything*! We all know He fulfilled the prophecies about the Messiah that are contained in Scripture. But what we often miss is that Jesus also dealt with, fulfilled and gave living example to all the customs and traditions of the people and even their superstitions.

For example, the Scriptures tell us that the Messiah would do healings and Jesus fulfilled that. One of the teachings of the Rabbis, though was that there would be healing in the "spittle" of the Messiah (8). This was certainly not a Scriptural teaching and yet Jesus performs at least one healing by putting His spit on the eyes of a blind man who is then healed and able to see. It doesn't matter how the Lord healed the man but He chose to perform that healing in a way that would even fulfill the traditions of the Rabbis.

Now Jesus does this in order to prevent anyone from saying "He cannot be the Messiah because He did not..." whatever. Jesus fulfilled everything. So when we come to Passover we see Jesus fulfilling all of the teachings and beliefs of the Jews concerning Passover and what the ultimate sacrifice of the Lamb of God would be – both those Scriptural teachings and the traditions of the Rabbis and customs of the people.

Before the arrival of Passover there is painstaking preparations taking place to cleanse the house of all leaven, which represents sin.

*Friday, Nissan 8* (6:00 Thursday night until 6:00 Friday night)
- Beginning of Kashering – spring cleaning – cleaning the house of leaven (I Corinthians 5:7-8, Exodus 12:15)
- Jesus arrives in Bethany to stay with Mary and Martha and Lazarus (John 12:1).
- Mary anoints Jesus for burial (John 12:1-8)

The next day the people are to spend time in worship to prepare themselves for the Passover and to focus their hearts on God and on the celebration.

*Saturday, Nissan 9* (6:00 Friday night until 6:00 Saturday night)
- *Sabbath*
- Jesus worships

Then comes the third day when the lambs for sacrifice are chosen and presented in the temple. They are examined by the priests for blemishes. The same day that the Jews were presenting their lambs to be inspected for the Passover we see our own Passover Lamb presenting himself to the people of Jerusalem and to the Priests in the Temple for inspection as the Lamb of God. The people accepted him but their leaders did not.

*Sunday, Nisan 10* (6:00 Saturday night until 6:00 Sunday night)
- Shabbat HaGadol - When the lambs are gathered in the temple for Passover (Exodus 12:3-5)
- Triumphal entry ending at the Temple (Zechariah 9:9, Matthew 21:1-11, Mark 11:1-11, Luke 19:28-44, John 12:12-15)

*"The disciples went and did as Jesus had instructed them. They brought the donkey and the colt, placed their cloaks on them, and Jesus sat on them. A very large crowd spread their cloaks on the road, while other cut branches from the trees and spread them on the road. [Crowd shouted Hosanna to the Son of David!] . . . Jesus entered the temple area . . .And he left them and went out of the city to Bethany, where he spent the night" (Matt 21:1-11 with a quote from Zechariah. 9:9)*

Approximately 50% of everything we read in the four Gospels takes place the last week of Jesus life before the crucifixion in the Temple courts and on the Mount of Olives. He is presenting Himself to the people and the priests for all to see who He truly is and that He is the unblemished sacrifice. He himself was then examined for 4 days by the chief priests, teachers of the law, Elders, Pharisees, Sadducees, and even Herodians, as He teaches, preaches, does miracles, etc. in and around the temple for the next four days. They could not find fault with him but would not accept Him as the Lamb of God and so, called on false witnesses in order to get him convicted.

*Monday, Nisan 11* (6:00 Sunday night until 6:00 Monday night)
- Caring for the lambs (Exodus 12:6)
- Clears the Temple of moneychangers (Matthew 21:12-17; Mark 11:15-26; Luke 19:45-48)

**Tuesday, Nisan 12** (6:00 Monday night until 6:00 Tuesday night)
- Caring for the lambs (Exodus 12:6)
- Cleanse the house of leaven again.
- Disputing with the Priests (Matthew 23)
- Teaching on the Mount of Olives (Matthew 12-25)

**Wednesday, Nisan 13** (Day before Passover - 6:00 Tues. night until 6:00 Wed. night)
- Caring for the lambs
- Ta'anit Bechorim - Fast of the First born sons (to remember those who were spared by the blood of the lamb in Egypt. And to mourn the death of the first born who perished. We must not rejoice over the death of our enemies. This was a tradition created by the Rabbis (9). Jesus rests and fasts according to custom fulfilling the tradition of the Rabbis).
- Bedikat Chametz – the last cleansing of leaven from the house, done by candlelight just after nightfall

On the fourth day all the people bring their lambs to the temple where they are sacrificed. Then the families take the lambs home, roast them in their entirety and eat them with Matzah (unleavened bread) and bitter herbs.

*Thursday, Nisan 14* (Feast of Passover - 6:00 Wednesday night until 6:00 Thurs. night)
- Twilight – slaughter the lambs for Passover (Exodus 12:6)
- Roast and eat the Passover lamb
- Passover meal with Jesus and Disciples – twilight
- Jesus changes Passover to Lord's supper
    - Fulfilling symbols of the daily sacrifice – Lamb & bread & wine (Mark 14:22-26)
    - Fulfilling symbols of the Passover – His blood will give us eternal life and cause the judgment of God to "pass over" us. (Exodus 12:13, Mark 14:24, I Peter 1:18,19)

- Changing the Passover sacrifice from an annual event to a once and for all event

The next day the people remember that this was the day when they first walked out of Egypt. This was the day when their deliverance from Egypt became a reality. They left carrying with them their unleavened bread. This represented leaving sin (leaven) behind in Egypt.

*Friday, Nisan 15* - Chag HaMatzot - Feast of Unleavened Bread - The day the Israelites were delivered from Egypt (Begins 6:00 Thursday. night until 6:00 on the 21st of Nissan, eight days later)
- Jesus betrayed, arrested and tried before Annas and Caiaphas and imprisoned – late Thurs. night (Friday according to lunar calendar) (Isaiah 53:3; Luke 3:2; John 18:13)
- Jesus tried before Sanhedrin, Pilate & Herod-1st hour of day - 6:00 - 7:00 a.m. (Isaiah 53:7,8)
- Jesus returned to Pilate, sentenced and beaten – 2nd hr of day – 7:00-8:00 am (Isaiah 53:5)
- Jesus led to Calvary and crucified – 3rd hour of the day – 9:00 a.m. (Psalm 22:1, 16-18, Isaiah 53:4,5)
- Jesus has died – 9th hour – 3:00 p.m. (Isaiah 53:8)
    This is when those who trust in Jesus alone for salvation left their sins behind and were delivered from eternal hell. The last sacrifice needed or accepted by the Heavenly Father has been accomplished and finished (10).
- Buried before sundown (before 6:00 on the 15th ) to avoid doing it on the Sabbath (Isaiah 53:9, 12)

This is when the people go to the temple to worship the Lord over the harvest they are about to reap and they pray He will give them a bountiful crop and thereby meet all their needs for survival. Here Jesus presents Himself to the Father as the first fruit of all those who will trust in Him for salvation. Jesus intercedes for us before the Heavenly Father to save us from eternal death

*Saturday, Nisan 16* - Sabbath - - Reishit Katzir - Feast of First Fruits (Begins 6:00 Friday night until 6:00 Sat. night) This is the day when the Jews remember when God delivered them from slavery and death.
- Jesus in the tomb, defeating the gates of hell and putting His own blood on the alter of the Heavenly Sanctuary

*Sunday, Nisan 17* (Begins 6:00 Saturday night until 6:00 Sunday night)
- The Jews remember the crossing of the Red Sea on this day when they were reborn from slaves to free men

- The Jews in Babylon fast for Queen Esther as she intercedes for the people before the King. She will either die or she will save them all from death.
- Jesus Resurrection! – Early morning before sunrise (Psalm 16:10, Isaiah 53:5,8,10-11, Acts 2:24) We are reborn from slaves to sin to children of God

Jesus in obedience to the Scriptures observed some of the above events. Some events, which He fulfilled, were prophetic. Some were customs and traditions. However, the greatest of all was when He fulfilled the Passover and turned it into the Lord's Supper or Communion. This, Jesus commands us to do until He comes again, because it is to remind us of His death on the cross as the Lamb of God and of His resurrection, which secured our salvation.

### How did Jesus Fulfill the Feast of Passover Meal?

The people at the table are seated in a special order. The leader reclines at the head of the table. This would have been Jesus. The youngest person sits at the right of the leader. This would have been John. A guest of honor would sit to the left of the leader. This would have been Judas based on the fact that he was sharing a bowl with Jesus (John 13:26-30).

The leader takes the *first cup of wine,* which is the Cup of Sanctification and while everyone is holding up their cup, he says a prayer. Jesus took the cup and gave thanks (Luke 22:17).

Then there is the *washing of hands*. It is at this point that Jesus washes the feet of the disciples and teaches them that He was the suffering servant and that He would be the one who would cleanse them eternally (John 13:4-5).

Then comes the *asking of the four questions* by the youngest member at the table. John would have asked the questions on this night and Jesus would have answered Him.

Next would be the *second cup of wine*, which is the Cup of Deliverance. The leader would recite the whole story of God's people from Abraham to Mt. Sinai. Then the first half of the Hallel is sung. Hallel means "praise" and has made its way into many languages as "Hallelujah" which means, "praise Jehovah". According to the Talmud the Levites sang this song in the temple as they were sacrificing the Passover lambs for each family. Here is Jesus the Lamb of God singing the Hallel over Himself as the Passover sacrifice.

Then comes the *Dipping of the Matzah* . Everyone takes two small pieces of Matzah cracker and puts a little bit of bitter herbs (or horseradish today) between. It must be enough to bring tears to your eyes in order to identify with your forefathers who were slaves in Egypt. It was at this time of remembering great suffering that Jesus tells the disciples that one of them will betray him (John 13:21-27).

At this point in the evening *a meal* is served. In Jesus day it would have literally been lamb, Matzah and bitter herbs. Today it is a meal with a great variety of kosher foods. By the time of the meal Judas had already left and did not eat with the rest.

It is at this point that we see that Jesus is the Lamb of God whose sacrifice delivers us eternally. The day after being questioned about whether he was the Christ, John the Baptist said when he saw Jesus approaching: "look, the Lamb of God, who takes away the sin of the world!" John later said that the Holy Spirit told him who Christ was and that He is "the Son of God". (John 1:29-34).

Now at that last Passover of the Lord and His disciples, Jesus illustrated that He is the Lamb of God by showing the disciples how He fulfilled the Passover and also how He fulfilled the daily sacrifices to God. At Mt. Sinai God gave the people instructions on all the feasts and festivals. He also gave them instructions on all the sacrifices to be given. One of these sacrifices was called the daily sacrifices and they were to be given every morning and every evening. The sacrifice to be given was an unblemished lamb, a measure of flour and oil mixed together (bread like substance) and wine. So here at Passover Jesus reveals that He is the Lamb of God the final and true sacrifice for the forgiveness of sins and He tells the disciples to remember the sacrifice He is about to make for them through the bread and the wine which represent His body and blood.

Later on, after the meal is the *third cup of wine*. This is the Cup of Redemption and is poured and sipped. This is the point where Jesus institutes the Lord's Supper (Luke 22:20). Jesus told the disciples how he had fulfilled the Passover and how He was the Cup of Redemption that would be poured out for His people. Using bread and the third cup He tells them that these are His body and blood and that they are to eat this until he comes again to remember His sacrifice for them.

Then the *fourth cup of wine*, which is the Cup of Acceptance or Praise, is poured and taken. This is also called the cup of the Kingdom and is based on God's fourth promise in Exodus 6:7 - *'Then I will take you for My people, and I will be your God; and you shall know that I am the LORD your God, who brought you out from under the burdens of the Egyptians.*

It is this cup that Jesus says He will not drink again until He drinks it with His disciples in the Kingdom (Matthew 26:29). The disciples thought this would be the time when Jesus would march on Jerusalem and take over as Messiah, but Jesus knew He had another cup He had to drink and He did not drink this one. Jesus said He would not drink this cup until He drank it with them in "My Father's Kingdom". In that day there will be a better feast – a feast for all those who have put their faith and trust in the Messiah (11)!

### *Conclusion*

After this night – no sacrifices would ever be needed by God again nor would any others ever be accepted. Jesus was the final and perfect sacrifice that was required by God to make all those who would receive Him as their Savior right and holy and pure before the Heavenly Father. Through Jesus sacrifice on the cross and His resurrection, our Heavenly Father kept His promise to us from Genesis 3:15 and made us one with Him in a holy and loving relationship once again and for all eternity.

Later that night Jesus went to the Garden – where He prayed. There He was betrayed and arrested and tried before Annas and Caiaphas the High Priest. In other words – He was the sacrificial lamb of God – brought to the temple to be slaughtered.

Early in the morning on Friday which was still considered Passover, Jesus was tried before Sanhedrin, Pilate & Herod (1st hour of day – 6:00-7:00 a.m.), returned to Pilate, sentenced and beaten (2nd hr of day – 7:00-8:00 am), and then led to Calvary and crucified (3rd hour of the day – 9:00 a.m.). Then He died (9th hour – 3:00 p.m.) and was buried before sundown. The Lamb of God had been sacrificed.

## Footnotes for Chapter Two:

1- RW Research, Inc. *Feast and Holidays of the Bible Pamphlet* ; Rose Publishing.
2- Irving Greenberg.  *The Jewish Way* . p. 25.
3- International Standard Bible Encyclopedia, p.543. and Francis Brown, S.R. Driver and C.A. Briggs.  Hebrew and English Lexicon of the Old Testament, p. 1.
4- Kevin Howard and Marvin Rosenthal.  *The Feasts of the Lord* .  p. 50.
5- Appendix #2.
6- http://www.blessisrael.net/Feasts%20and%20Festivals.htm
7- Kevin Howard and Marvin Rosenthal.  *The Feasts of the Lord* .  p. 54.
8- George Konig.  *Christian Internet Forum* .  www.konig.org.
9- John J. Parsons.  *Hebrew for Christians* . hebrew4christians.com.
10- *The Bible Visual Resource Book* .  p. 193.
11- Joan R. Lipis.  *Celebrate the Haggadah* .  p. 47.  The whole section on the Passover meal comes from this book.

# Chapter Three - Sanctification
## Chag Ha Matzot - Feast of Unleavened Bread (Nisan 15)

*"The Lamb of God had been sacrificed and buried."*

*6 On the fifteenth day of that month the LORD's Feast of Unleavened Bread begins; for seven days you must eat bread made without yeast. 7 On the first day hold a sacred assembly and do no regular work. 8 For seven days present an offering made to the LORD by fire. And on the seventh day hold a sacred assembly and do no regular work.' " Leviticus 23:6-8*
*"Therefore purge out the old leaven, that you may be a new lump, since you truly are unleavened. For indeed Christ, our Passover was sacrificed for us.8. Therefore let us keep the feast, not with old leaven, nor with the leaven of malice and wickedness, but with the unleavened bread of sincerity and truth." 1 Corinthians 5: 7,8.*

The Feast of Unleavened Bread is one of the most joyous festivals in the life of God's people. Just as we remember the sadness and horror of our Savior's death in the light of His glorious and joyous resurrection, we remember the sadness of slavery (and sin) in the light of the joy of our deliverance. This is not a feast to remember Israel's bondage but rather to remember her deliverance from bondage. For the Christian it celebrates our deliverance from sin. The unleavened bread, the badge of former affliction became the symbol of a new and joyous life, in which the people were to devote themselves and all that they had unto the Lord (1).

Sometimes confused with Passover, the Feast of Unleavened Bread, while directly linked to the Passover is actually a feast on its own. As they prepared to leave Egypt the Lord commanded the Israelites to remove all traces of leaven from their homes. Biblically, this leaven is symbolic of sin, and as Death was set to pass over the homes with blood on the doorposts, the lack of leaven in those homes would further signify their "righteousness."

The unleavened bread, eaten with the roasted Passover Lamb on the evening of the fourteenth day of the first month further signified the suddenness with which the Israelites' deliverance would come. The bread simply did not have the time to rise before they had to eat it and go. " *And they baked unleavened cakes of the dough which they had brought out of Egypt; for it was not leavened, because they were driven out of Egypt and could not wait, nor had they prepared provisions for themselves"* (Exodus 12:39).

In Israel today, those keeping this feast purchase enormous packs of special "Kosher for Passover" unleavened bread called *Matzah* from the supermarkets. All non-kosher for Passover products, including corn flakes, pop corn, beer, potato crisps, beans etc. are covered up for the duration of the week. Ordinary bread is nowhere to be found. The number of menu items, which use matzo flour, is quite impressive. The novelty of the light and crisp crackers quickly wears off, however, and Israelis soon start referring to *Matzot* as the "bread of affliction (2)." Passover and the Feast of Unleavened Bread are the first two feasts that God gives; instituting them before the people left Egypt (Leviticus 12).

### When is the Feast of Unleavened Bread?

The seven-day Feast of Unleavened Bread begins on the evening of Passover, a one-day feast. Because this feast begins the very next day after Passover the two are often combined and called "the eight days of Passover". In Jesus day it was common to call these eight days the Feast of Unleavened Bread (Luke 22:1,7). However they are separate holidays with Passover being on the 14th of Nisan and Unleavened Bread beginning on the 15th of Nisan.

The feast was not one of the three pilgrim feasts of Israel, however, Passover was and with this feast beginning the very next day, the majority of the pilgrims to the temple would have still been in Jerusalem for this feast as well. A Pilgrim feast was when every male in Israel had to go to the Temple to celebrate the particular festival. Many of them would have brought their families. Hundreds of thousands of people would have flooded Jerusalem and the villages all around it as well as camping all over the Mount of Olives. The other Pilgrim feasts were Pentecost and Tabernacles.

In keeping this commandment Jesus would have traveled to Jerusalem for each of the Pilgrim feasts each year of His life on earth. It was during the Feast of Unleavened Bread, according to Luke 2:42-43, 46-47, that Jesus remained behind in the temple at age 12 and astonished all who heard Him with His knowledge of the things of God.

### What Is the Feast of Unleavened Bread?

The Feast of Unleavened Bread is a time for putting away leaven and keeping it out of lives. What does leaven symbolize? It symbolizes sin or pride, because it puffs up our hearts as well as our bread. You can't see leaven and you can't see sin itself but you can see the results of both as they work themselves out – leaven making the bread rise and sin revealing our rebellion against God in our thoughts, words and deeds. Paul says in I Corinthians 5:6-8, *"Your boasting is not good Do you not know that a little leaven leavens the whole lump of dough? Clean out the old leaven so that you may be a new lump, just as you are in fact unleavened. For Christ our Passover also has been sacrificed. Therefore let us celebrate the feast, not with old leaven, nor with the leaven of malice and wickedness, but with the unleavened bread of sincerity and truth. "* Then Paul speaks in connection with the Lord's Supper and says in I Corinthians 11:28 " *But a man must examine himself, and in so doing he is to eat of the bread and drink of the cup .*" We must put away sin from our lives, all of our lives.

It is a reminder and a memorial of God's miraculous deliverance of the people from slavery in Egypt, when they had to flee in the middle of the night after Death had passed over the land. Deuteronomy 3:16 says *"You shall not eat leavened bread with it; seven days you shall eat with it unleavened bread, the bread of affliction (for you came out of the land of Egypt in haste), so that you may remember all the days of your life the day when you came out of the land of Egypt. "* And Exodus 12:39 says *"They baked the dough, which they had brought out of Egypt into cakes of unleavened bread. For it had not become leavened, since they were driven out of Egypt and could not delay, nor had they prepared any provisions for themselves. "*

Unleavened bread (matzah) had been the mark of Israel's affliction and bondage and subjection to the Egyptians to the point that even in leaving Egypt, they were essentially driven out of Egypt with great haste (Deut. 16:3; Exodus 12:33,39). This was such a big part of the remembrance of the Exodus that Isaiah refers to it when he speaks to the people of a much greater deliverance in 52:11-12. *"Depart, depart, go out from there, touch nothing unclean; go out of the midst of her, purify yourselves, you who carry the vessels of the LORD. But you will not go out in haste, nor will you go as fugitives; For the LORD will go before you, and the God of Israel will be your rear guard"* (3).

Unleavened bread is also the symbol of moral corruption and of sin. It was to represent Israel staying away from these things for seven days (a symbolic number signifying completeness) to teach that the redeemed must separate themselves from evil and be a holy people. This feast is about our lifelong struggle in sanctification, which is seeking to live a life pleasing to our God (4).

### What is the Meaning of the Feast of Unleavened Bread?

The Feast of Unleavened Bread is a week of *sanctification*, being especially set apart for God, to be holy as He is holy. It is a time for putting away leaven or *sin* and keeping it out of lives. This feast represents our *sanctification* as we rid ourselves of the old leaven of "Egypt" and die to the old nature. In fact, this is represented by the burial of Jesus and our identification with His death **(5).**

The Lord Christ Jesus was crucified on the cross at Golgotha on the day of Passover. He was then buried in a newly hewn tomb donated by Joseph of Arimathea. However, unlike all other corpses, the body of Jesus would not decay in the grave. There would be no decomposition of His body, none at all. God the Father would not *"allow your Holy One (His Son Jesus) to see corruption"* (Psalm 16:10; Acts 2:27). The Feast of Unleavened Bread proclaims that Christ's physical body would not experience the ravages of death while in the grave for God the Father sanctified him (6).

Now sanctification is something that God does in us, when we yield to His Spirit. Psalm 139: 23 says, *"Search me, O God, and know my heart; test me and know my anxious thoughts. 24 See if there is any offensive way in me, and lead me in the way everlasting. "* However, we are called to have a part in this process and so in Philippians 2:12, the apostle urges us to *"continue to work out your salvation with fear and trembling, for it is God who works in you to will and to act according to his good purpose."* God in Jesus is working to bring about sanctification, for I cannot make myself holy. Nevertheless, I must cooperate, by continuing to work out my salvation. And the starting point for getting my will motivated is what the Bible calls *"the fear of the Lord."* Proverbs 16:6, declares, *"By the fear of the Lord men depart from evil."* Sin has consequences, and every one of us will have to deal with those consequences.

But thanks be to God, Proverbs 16:6 also says, *"through love and faithfulness sin is atoned for."* Whose love? Jesus' love! Jesus' love covers a multitude of sins! *"Though your sins are like scarlet, they shall be as white as snow."* As Hebrews 10:13 says, *"by one sacrifice he has made perfect forever those who are being made holy."* We have a calling to work out our salvation but apart from the atoning work of Jesus on our behalf, this is impossible for us to accomplish.

### *How was the Feast of Unleavened Bread to be celebrated?*

The Bible only gives three instructions for this feast. The first is that special sacrifices were to be offered in the temple each day of the feast. According to Numbers 28 these sacrifices were:

v. 19 - two young bulls, one ram and seven male lambs

v. 20 - with each bull prepare a grain offering of three-tenths of an ephah of fine flour mixed with oil; with the ram, two-tenths; 21 and with each of the seven lambs, one-tenth.

v. 22 - include one male goat as a sin offering to make atonement for you.

v. 23 - prepare these in addition to the regular morning burnt offering(s of two lambs a year old without defect, together with a grain offering of a tenth of an ephah of fine flour mixed with a quarter of a hin of oil from pressed olives).

The second instruction for the feast was the first and last days of the feast (Nisan 15 and Nisan 21) were to be special Sabbath days with prohibitions on all work (Exodus 12:16; Lev. 23:7-8; Num. 28:25 and Deut. 16:8). The third instruction was that all leaven was strictly forbidden. The Scriptures strongly emphasize the prohibition of leaven during this feast. This prohibition is so strong that the Jews came to teach that you could not even have anything with leaven in it in your house during this festival. The feast days would begin before Nisan 15 with the search and removal of all leaven from the homes of those celebrating the feast. Exodus 12:15 says that if anyone eats anything with leaven in it during these days he shall be cut off from Israel (7)!

### *How was the Feast of Unleavened Bread Celebrated in Jesus day?*

This feast was to be a very joyous feast and was not to be a burden on the people. The first day of the feast was considered to be a High Sabbath and no unnecessary work could be done. Now, there were many sacrifices to be given on the first day of the feast. Some were to be given by the nation, some by the people and some by individuals. But they were all designed to bring joy to the people. The public or national sacrifices were to be given for the forgiveness of sins, which brought spiritual joy to the people. The sacrifices of the people were called "peace offerings"**(8)** to represent a loving relationship between the people and God, and the sacrifices of the individuals were called "offerings of joyousness" according to the blessings that God had given to each of them. All of these sacrifices were to be based on what the people could easily afford however. They were not to be burdensome or cause struggle to a family. This was not to be a heavy yoke of bondage but a joyous festival.

It is interesting to note that the peace offerings could not be given by anyone who had contracted Levitical defilement (9). This is why the Jews that led Jesus from Caiaphas into the hall of judgment did not want to go in. John 18:28 says *"Then they led Jesus from Caiaphas into the Praetorium, and it was early; and they themselves did not enter into the Praetorium so that they would not be defiled, but might eat the Passover."*

The Matzah is the symbol of the Feast of Unleavened Bread. It is a reminder of the bread the people had to eat the night before they left Egypt. But it is also a symbol of the feast. This bread would have been a sign to the people, most certainly the children, that this was a special time in the life of God's people. Special activities and teachings were going to happen at this time. There was an air of joyful expectation. And every day had special remembrances, activities, teachings and significance (10).

26

Additionally, the people remember and celebrated certain events in their history each day. The celebration of the Feast of Unleavened Bread would have had the following schedule (all year dates are according to Jewish teachings):

### Nisan 15 - Yom Tov - High Sabbath
1- This was a festival Sabbath – if Nisan 15 fell on any day other than the weekly Saturday Sabbath, there would be two Sabbaths that week.

2- The *Yom Tov* days are days of rest, during which all creative work is forbidden, as it is on the Sabbath, with the exception of certain types of work associated with food preparation (e.g., cooking and "carrying").

3- On this day the people commemorate:
- Covenant between God and Abraham that is made by the Lord walking between the halves of the sacrificial animals that God makes with (1743 BC)
- Abraham battles the four kings (1738 BC)
- Angels visit Abraham (1714 BC)
- Isaac is born (1713 BC)
- Jacob wrestles with the Angel (1556 BC)
- God speaks to Moses at the burning bush (1314 BC)
- The Beginning of the Exodus (1313 BC)
- Daniel in the Lions Den (372 BC) **(11)**

4- Begin the Omer Count (counting 50 days to the Festival of Weeks {Pentecost})

### Nisan 16 - The Feast of First Fruits
1- This was the third Spring Feast of Israel, which we will cover, in the next chapter.

2- On this day the people commemorate:
Sodom Overturned (1714 BC)
The first day that there was no manna after they entered the Promised Land (1273 BC)
Esther appears before the King (357 BC)

3- Second day of counting Omer

### Nisan 17 - Chol Hamoed – Intermediate Days
1- The middle four days of the Feast are called *chol hamoed* "weekdays of the festival," also called "the intermediate days." On *chol hamoed* the prohibition of work is less stringent--work whose avoidance would result in "significant loss" is permitted (except when *chol hamoed* is also Sabbath, when all work is forbidden).

2- On this day the people commemorate:

The day that Haaman was killed and the Jews in Persia were
saved by Queen Esther (357 BC)

    3- Third day of counting Omer

### Nisan 18 - Chol Hamoed – Intermediate Days
1- Fourth day of counting Omer

### Nisan 19 - Chol Hamoed – Intermediate Days
1- Fifth day of counting Omer

### Nisan 20 - Chol Hamoed – Intermediate Days
1- On this day the people celebrate a night of learning. They stay up the
whole night reading and studying God's word. It is customary
to remain awake on the eve of the Seventh of Passover (i.e.,
tonight) and spend the entire night in Torah study.

2- The people have a joyous celebration to commemorate the great
miracle of the splitting of the sea. (1313 BC)

3- Sixth day of counting Omer.

### Nisan 21 - Yom Tov - High Sabbath
1- This was a festival Sabbath – if Nisan 21 fell on any day other than
the weekly Saturday Sabbath, there would be two Sabbaths that
week.

2- The *Yom Tov* days are days of rest, during which all creative work is
forbidden, as it is on the Shabbat, with the exception of certain
types of work associated with food preparation (e.g., cooking
and "carrying").

3- *Yizkor,* the remembrance prayer for departed parents, is recited today
after the morning reading of the Torah.

4- On this day the people commemorate:
    Moses departing Midian (1314 BC)

5- The Messiah's Meal - The last day of Passover is particularly
associated with the Messiah and the future redemption.

6- Seventh day of counting Omer (Omer is continued to be counted
even after the Feast ends until the Fest of Pentecost) (12).

### How did Jesus Fulfill the Feast of Unleavened Bread?

Passover pictures the substitutionary death of the Messiah as the
Passover Lamb. The Prophets spoke of the day when the Messiah would be a
sacrifice for sin. He would be the Lamb offered up to God and by God as the
once-for-all sacrifice. Isaiah says *"4Surely our griefs He Himself bore, and our
sorrows He carried; yet we ourselves esteemed Him stricken, Smitten of God,
and afflicted. 6All of us like sheep have gone astray, each of us has turned to his*

*own way; But the LORD has caused the iniquity of us all to fall on Him.* **10** *But the LORD was pleased to crush Him, putting Him to grief; If He would render Himself as a guilt offering, He will see His offspring, He will prolong His days, and the good pleasure of the LORD will prosper in His hand"* (53:4,6,10).

The Feast of Unleavened Bread pictures the burial of the Messiah. The prophets also spoke about the Messiah's amazing burial. Once again Isaiah 53 says *"9His grave was assigned with wicked men, Yet He was with a rich man in His death, Because He had done no violence, Nor was there any deceit in His mouth".*

Normally when one dies a criminal's death he is given a criminals burial. But this was not what happened to Jesus. Jesus was executed as though he was a criminal but God did not allow his body to be cast outside the city onto the garbage heap. He died not for His own sins because He had none. Rather he died for our sins for we are all guilty. Therefore God honored Him with a burial in the tomb of a rich man, Joseph of Arimathea, a member of the Sanhedrin (Mt. 27:57-60). This was God's statement on the innocence of Jesus (13).

But we are also told that messiah's body would not *"return to the dust".* *David* prophesied about the Messiah when he said in Psalm 16:10 " *10For You will not abandon my soul to Sheol; Nor will You allow Your Holy One to undergo decay."* All of us as descendants of Adam are under the curse to die and have our bodies return to the dust. But as a pure, sinless sacrifice the Messiah was not under this curse.

The Messiah fulfilled the feast in that He was a pure sinless (without leaven) sacrifice. God the Father validates this by having Jesus buried in the tomb of a rich man. And then His body was not permitted to decay but was resurrected because He was not a sinner under the curse of death and decay.

### *Conclusion*

I Corinthians 5:7-8 says *"7Clean out the old leaven so that you may be a new lump, just as you are in fact unleavened. For Christ our Passover also has been sacrificed. 8Therefore let us celebrate the feast, not with old leaven, nor with the leaven of malice and wickedness, but with the unleavened bread of sincerity and truth."* Paul's message is simple. For those who have, by faith, accepted the Passover Lamb at Calvary, Passover is past history. Their Feast of Passover, their deliverance by the Messiah has already been experienced in their lives.

But now they are living in the Feast of Unleavened Bread where purity and separation from leaven or sin is required. Paul is stating to the Corinthians what he would later write to the Romans in 6:1-18. The believer is no longer under the power of sin. Sin's power over him has been broken. The believer is no longer controlled by sin but still commits sin. All this means that we can also have victory over sin. In God's sight we are now justified (unleavened) and are called to lives of holiness. The outworking and living of this life of holiness is called sanctification, based on the work of Christ in His death, burial and resurrection. It is accomplished through the grace of Christ and by the power of the Holy Spirit.

To live in the Feast of Unleavened Bread (Sanctification), we must live every day as the Jews sought to live only at Passover time. We are to strive to cast out the leaven (sin) in our lives and hearts every day. Why? *"For Christ our Passover also has been sacrificed" (I Corinthians 5:7).*

# Footnotes for Chapter Three:

1- Alfred Edershiem. *The Temple* . p. 166.

2- Stan Goodenough. *Chag HaMatzot - Unleavened Bread.* israelmybeloved.com.

3- Alfred Edershiem. *The Temple* . p. 166.

4- J. Sidlow Baxter. *Explore the Book* . p.140.

5- Alfred Edershiem. *The Temple* . p. 166.

6- http://christcenteredmall.com/teachings/feasts/unleavened-bread.htm

7- The Requirements Directing the Feast of Unleavened Bread (Lev. 23:6; Ex. 12:15-17):

    A) The first day, all leaven should be removed from the home (Ex. 12:15).

    B) For seven days they were to eat unleavened bread (Lev. 23:6, Ex. 12:15).

    C) This feast was a high Sabbath (an extra Sabbath besides the weekly Sabbath). No work should be done the first day and the seventh day (except preparing food) (Ex. 12:16).

    D) This feast was declared a memorial to be kept forever. And ye shall observe the feast of unleavened bread... therefore shall ye observe this day in your generations by an ordinance for ever (Ex. 12:17).

8- Derech Ministries. http://www.derech.org/index2.html

9- *Mishnah* , Pesahim 6:3.

10- Alfred Edershiem. *Sketches of Jewish Life* . p. 103.

11- *Chabad.Org Calendar*. chabad.org/calendar/view/day.htm/aid/142130/ jewish/Jewish- Calendar. This is a calendar that shares are the dates of the entire Jewish history. All the dates I have included in this book from Creation to the end of the Old Testament were found on this calendar.

12- Appendix Number Four

13- Kevin Howard and Marvin Rosenthal. *The Feasts of the Lord* . p. 70

# Chapter Four - Adoption
## Ha Bikkurim- Feast of First Fruits *(Nisan 16)*

*His body was not permitted to decay but was resurrected because He was not a sinner under the curse of death and decay.*

*9Then the LORD spoke to Moses, saying, 10"Speak to the sons of Israel and say to them, 'When you enter the land which I am going to give to you and reap its harvest, then you shall bring in the sheaf of the first fruits of your harvest to the priest. 11He shall wave the sheaf before the LORD for you to be accepted; on the day after the Sabbath the priest shall wave it.*

*12 Now on the day when you wave the sheaf, you shall offer a male lamb one year old without defect for a burnt offering to the LORD. 13Its grain offering shall then be two-tenths of an ephah of fine flour mixed with oil, an offering by fire to the LORD for a soothing aroma, with its drink offering, a fourth of a hin of wine.*

*14Until this same day, until you have brought in the offering of your God, you shall eat neither bread nor roasted grain nor new growth. It is to be a perpetual statute throughout your generations in all your dwelling places.*

*15You shall also count for yourselves from the day after the Sabbath, from the day when you brought in the sheaf of the wave offering; there shall be seven complete Sabbaths. (Leviticus 23:9-15)*

Often overlooked because Passover and the Feast of Unleavened Bread over shadow and surround it, the Feast of First Fruits can nonetheless be called the most important Feast of them all, at least from a Christian point of view. This is because it was on the Feast of First Fruits that the Lord Jesus rose from the dead and sealed our salvation for all eternity. This is the most important feast, even though the Gospel accounts don't even mention First Fruits and also seem to use Passover and Unleavened Bread interchangeably. It's easy to miss the fact that there were actually three feasts being celebrated at once. It's even easier to miss the significance of Christ rising from the dead on this day.

There are actually two first fruits. The early first fruits celebration that occurs the day following the High Sabbath after Passover (or the second day after Passover) is considered Early First fruits. Fifty days later the latter second first fruits occur, called the Feast of Weeks (Pentecost). The fifty days in between are called The Counting of the Omer (1).

### When is the Feast of First Fruits?

To repeat - This Feast is the third Spring Feast and falls during the week of the Feast of Unleavened Bread on the day after the High Sabbath (the High Sabbath is on Nisan 15 and First Fruits is on Nisan 16). This is the feast of the early first fruits and is also known as "the Counting of the Sheaf" (or Omer). It speaks of the earliest harvest that takes place in Israel, the barley harvest (2).

In Leviticus 23, this day is called B'Yom Haneefchem Et Ha Omer, "The Day You Bring in the Sheaf of the Wave Offering". God commanded the people, once they got to the Promised Land, to bring the first fruits of their barley harvest as a wave offering (Lev.23: 11) before Him on this day (Lev.23: 10).

An interesting side note is that the Jewish calendar has several events of Biblical history taking place on this day. They believe that Sodom and Gomorrah were destroyed on this day in 1714 BC; that Manna stopped coming on this day in 1273 BC; and that Queen Esther appeared unsummoned before the King in order to save the Jews of Persia in 357 BC. In the Bible itself we are told that Ruth and Naomi arrive in Bethlehem from Moab on the Feast of First Fruits (Ruth 1:22). Also, that the day that King David made peace with the Gibeonites after King Saul had tried to kill them was on the Feast of First Fruits (2 Samuel 21:9). And in I Kings 4:21 and I Chronicles 9:26 we are told the boundaries of Israel in Solomon's day by telling how far the Feast of Unleavened Bread (including First Fruits) was celebrated in Israel (3). The connection between Jesus ancestors, the city of Bethlehem, the Feast of First Fruits and Jesus Himself is a long running one.

### *First Fruits and Easter*

The year the Lord was crucified, Passover fell on a Thursday. Three days and three nights later it was Sunday morning, the Feast of First Fruits. And for several hundred years after that, Christians knew the Sunday morning after Passover as Resurrection Morning.

Later, at the Council of Nicea in 325 A.D., Eastern and Western Bishops of the Church disagreed over the official date for the Church's most important Holy Day. Eastern Bishops favored staying with the calculation involving Passover as Leviticus describes, since many of them were of Jewish origin, and since the Gospels had placed Resurrection Morning just after Passover.

Western Bishops, being mostly Gentile, favored a date closer to the beginning of spring because there were already a number of pagan festivals held during that time and a religious holiday would fit right in. It is thought that perhaps this is when the Western Church began referring to Resurrection Morning as Easter Sunday, after the Babylonian fertility goddess Ishtar. The Feast of Ishtar was always celebrated at the beginning of spring and involved eggs and rabbits and other signs of fertility. Even today, you can see how elements of the two have been merged together (4).

Eventually, due in part to their view that since the Jews had rejected Christ, Jewish traditions shouldn't be used in selecting the date for Easter, the Western Church settled on the first Sunday after the first full moon after the spring equinox. Soon Easter Sunday became disconnected from Passover and the Feast of First Fruits by as much as several weeks.

### *What Is the Feast of First Fruits?*

First Fruits was a national observance, but each family brought its respective offerings to the Temple as well. Early each spring the farmers performed the ritual of setting their first fruits apart. The farmers and their families went into the fields to mark the best of their unripened crops. A rush or a cord was tied carefully around the selected first fruits so as not to damage them. Excitement would mount in the family as the first fruits ripened and were finally harvested for the Passover Pilgrimage to Jerusalem.

Grains were planted in the fall in Israel. They germinated in the ground through the winter, shot up as soon as the weather got warm, and ripened in the spring, barley first and then wheat. The first sheaf of barley or first fruits of the harvest is subsequently cut. But eating any of the grain was not permitted until a sample sheaf was brought to the Temple in a carefully prescribed and meticulous ceremony, at sunrise on the first day after the High Sabbath following Passover and is presented to the Lord. The Lord's acceptance of the First Fruits is a pledge on His part of a full harvest to come. A similar ceremony for the wheat harvest took place on Pentecost, also a Sunday, seven weeks (a total of 50 days) later (5).

The priest took the sheaf of grain and waved it before the altar of the Lord as a sample of the harvest. This was called the "wave offering". The people gave the wave offering to the Lord. The Lord then gave His portion to the Priests. This is in contrast to the "heave offering". The people gave the heave offering directly to the Priests. Both offerings were for the care and sustenance of the Priests (6).

To be sure the wave offering was acceptable to the Lord, a year old lamb was also offered, along with about 4 quarts of a flour and oil mixture and a quart of wine. The mixing fragrances of the roasting lamb, the baking bread dough and the steam from the wine made a pleasant aroma for the Lord and the offering was accepted. The Lord having received His required first portion, the harvest could proceed and the grain could be ground into flour for their daily bread.

34

Here again we see the symbolism of the lamb, the bread and the wine. These three found their fulfillment in Jesus that Lamb of God who gives us bread and wine as His body and blood to cover us with His grace and keep our eyes on Him until He returns to take us to live with Him forever.

### *What is the Meaning of the Feast of First Fruits?*

Historically, this was the day that the Hebrews went down into the Red Sea and emerged alive on the other side after God had parted the waters and allowed them to cross over on dry land. Later that morning, when the Egyptians were allowed to enter in after the Hebrews, God caused the water to return to its normal state, killing Pharaoh's army and ending the Egyptian rights of ownership of the children of Israel.

According to Genesis 47:13-26, Pharaoh owned all the people of Egypt except the Egyptian priests, which would include the Jewish slaves. In order for the children of Israel to go to the Promised Land, they would have to be set free from the Pharaoh's ownership. Moses, following God's instruction, had only requested of Pharaoh that the people be allowed to go three days journey into the wilderness to hold a feast unto God. Pharaoh transgressed his own commandment of allowing the people to go by pursuing them before the three days were over. If Pharaoh had waited until the end of the three days, Moses would have returned with the people, for God cannot and will not lie. But now Egypt no longer had a claim over the children of Israel and they were free to continue on to the Promise Land.

Now ceremonially, because of all the Lord did in bringing the people out of Egypt He claims for Himself the first fruits of everything. God declared that the first fruits of all agricultural produce belonged to Him from grain to wine to oil to fleece (Exodus 22:29; 23:19; Deut. 18:4; 26:2). This included all the seven major crops of Israel: barley, wheat, grapes, figs, pomegranates, olives and dates. Further still, all the firstborn males of all animals belonged to God (Exodus 22:30, Lev. 27:26), and indeed, even the firstborn of the Israelites themselves, belonged to Him (Exodus 13:2, 12-15; 34:19-20; Num. 3:13; 18:15-16).

It is very interesting to see how Jesus fulfilled so many of the concepts connected with being the first fruits that belong to God. Some of the ways Jesus did this are in His being...
    the firstborn of Mary (Matthew 1:23-25),
    the first and only begotten of God the Father (Hebrews 1:6),
    the firstborn of every creature (Colossians 1:15),
    the first-begotten from the dead (Revelation 1:5),

the firstborn of many brethren (Romans 8:29),
the first fruits of the resurrected ones (1 Corinthians 15:20,23),
the beginning of the creation of God (Revelation 3:14),
the preeminent One (Colossians 1:18).

Jesus is indeed the Most Holy One of God and is sanctified by the Father. He is the first, the choicest, the preeminent One. He is both the firstborn of God, and the first fruits unto God. Jesus is indeed, the ultimate sheaf of the first fruits. Since God accepted the sacrifice of Jesus' First Fruits there will be a full harvest of the followers of Jesus to come. When we place our trust in Christ alone for salvation we become part of the full harvest that will be gathered in to the Kingdom of Heaven and into the family of God by the Heavenly Father.

Ultimately the Feast of First Fruits is a time marker. It marked the beginning of the grain harvest, but even more importantly it marked the beginning of the countdown to the Feast of Weeks (Pentecost) Israel's fourth and last spring feast. Lev. 23:15 says: "You shall also count for yourselves from the day after the Sabbath, from the day when you brought in the sheaf of the wave offering; there shall be seven complete Sabbaths."

For Christians it is also a time marker. It marks the time from the Resurrection of the Lord until the day when the Holy Spirit came to be our comforter and to live with us until Jesus comes again. It marks the extended time from the Resurrection of Christ until His glorious Second Coming. The Feast of First Fruits is the first harvest – the Resurrection of the Lord. It marks the time until the second harvest, the thousands converted on the day of Pentecost. It marks the time until the final harvest when all those who have been adopted into the family of God will be gathered into heaven for eternity.

### How was the Feast of First Fruits to be celebrated?

The Biblical regulations for this feast are outlined in Lev. 23:9-14. A sheaf ("omer" meaning measure) was to be brought to the priests at the temple who would wave it before the Lord for acceptance. There were also to be accompanying sacrifices; an unblemished male lamb one year old, a drink offering of wine and a meal offering of the barley flour mixed with oil. To neglect these offerings was considered robbery of God according to Scripture (Malachi 3:8) (7). Deuteronomy 26:1-10 tells us the full ritual ceremony or the Feast of First Fruits (see Appendix #5).

On the Mount of Olives, in an area known as Ashes Valley, there was a small field of barley. This was a special field cultivated solely for the national First Fruits offering and kept in accordance with all rabbinic traditions. This crop was grown all naturally with no artificial watering or fertilization. At the beginning of First Fruits, a three-man delegation from the Sanhedrin emerged from the Temple and was followed by a procession of the people over to the field. Previously selected and bound sheaves were then harvested, with a great deal of ceremony. The Rabbis depose as follows, according to the citations of Dr. Lightfoot. *"The sheaf of first fruits was reaped from the Ashes Valley of Kedron. The first day of the feast of the First Fruits, certain persons deputed from the Sanhedrin went forth into that valley, a great company attending them, and very many of the neighboring towns flocked together that the thing might be done—a great number being present. They performed the thing with as much show as could be. When it was now evening, he, on whom the office of reaping laid, saith: 'The sun is set.' And they answered, 'Well.' 'With this reaping hook.' And they answered, 'Well; with this reaping hook.' 'In this basket.' And they answered, 'Well.' 'On this Sabbath.' And they answered, 'Well.' 'I will reap.' And they answered, 'Well, I will reap.' And they answered, 'Well.' This he said thrice; and they answered thrice, 'Well.' (8).' "*

Then the flour was threshed and sifted to a specific consistency. The Temple Treasurer then had to stick his hand in the flour. If any flour stuck to his hand it had to be sifted some more (9). The offering included the prayer from Deuteronomy 26:3,5,9-10. *3"You shall go to the priest who is in office at that time and say to him, 'I declare this day to the LORD my God that I have entered the land which the LORD swore to our fathers to give us. 5"You shall answer and say before the LORD your God, My father was a wandering Aramean, and he went down to Egypt and sojourned there, few in number; but there he became a great, mighty and populous nation. 9and He has brought us to this place and has given us this land, a land flowing with milk and honey. 10Now behold, I have brought the first of the produce of the ground, which You, O LORD have given me. And you shall set it down before the LORD your God, and worship before the LORD your God."*

The Jewish observance of this feast has varied over the centuries. In ancient practice, in the days of the Temple, it was quite an elaborate ceremony involving bringing the offerings as a thanksgiving tithe to God. The Talmud states that a priest would meet a group of Jewish pilgrims on the edge of the city and lead them up to the Temple Mount. As they carried their offerings of the first fruits, the priest would lead a praise service with music, praise, psalms and dance (10).

As the group of worshipers arrived at the Temple compound, the priest would take the sheaves, lift some in the air and wave them in every direction. By doing so, the whole crowd would be acknowledging God's provision and sovereignty over all the earth. The lesson of First Fruits is clear: if God has been faithful to bless us with this early harvest, He will most certainly provide the harvest of later summer.

The modern synagogue observance of First Fruits is fairly simple. While in the Temple period it involved offerings, processions and praise services, the contemporary celebration consists primarily of prayers and blessings from the Jewish Siddur (prayer book). These help people reflect on the symbolic meaning of the day, counting the days ("omer") from the barley to the wheat harvest at Shavuot (Pentecost), the next major feast.

God commanded the counting of the Omer. *"You shall count for yourselves -- from the day after the Shabbat, from the day when you bring the Omer of the waving -- seven Shabbats, they shall be complete. Until the day after the seventh Sabbath you shall count, fifty days..."* -Leviticus 23:15-16. *"You shall count for yourselves seven weeks; from when the sickle is first put to the standing crop shall you begin counting seven weeks. Then you will observe the Festival of Pentecost for the Lord, your God."* (Deuteronomy 16:9-10)

Many Jews begin the counting of the omer on the first day of the Feast of Unleavened Bread, with the reading of the traditional blessing: "Blessed art thou, O Lord our God, King of the universe, who has set us apart by your commandments and has commanded us concerning the counting of the sheaf."

This blessing is read every evening for the next forty-nine days, with an adjustment made according to the number of days that have been counted. For example: "Today is the first day of the sheaf". The next day would be the second day, then the third, then the fourth and so on. The fiftieth day marks the Feast of Pentecost. The blessings and numbering of the omer can be found in most Jewish Siddurs. Some people even make use of a special calendar to help keep track to the appropriate day.

### *The Counting of the Omer – Journey to Mount Sinai*

After crossing the Red Sea, the children of Israel traveled forty-seven days until they reached the mountain of God, Mount Sinai. They then spent three days of separation, preparing themselves to go before God and receive the Torah. This date would establish the date of the fourth feast for the Israelites (Lev.23:16-22). The forty-seven days of traveling and then three days of preparation before going before God exactly parallels the fifty days between the Resurrection of Jesus and the giving of the Holy Spirit on the Feast of Pentecost.

An interesting thought regarding the number of people who were killed because of their disobedience (Israel) and the number saved on the Day of Pentecost. When the Torah (Law) was given on Mount Sinai, three thousand people lost their lives through their disobedience and idolatry (Exodus 32:28). When the Holy Spirit came on the Feast of Pentecost and Peter preached the message of salvation through Jesus, three thousand people accepted Jesus as their Messiah and Savior and were saved (Acts 2:41).

### *How did Jesus Fulfill the Feast of First Fruits?*

At sunrise on the morning of the Feast of First Fruits in 32 AD, as the priests were waving the sheaf of grain before the altar, the women arrived at the Lord's tomb to prepare His body for permanent burial. Remember, there wasn't enough time before sunset on the day He was crucified and the next day was the Sabbath, so no work was permitted. (Interestingly, work was permitted on the Feast of First Fruits, although not on Pentecost.) But the tomb was empty. He had risen, the First Fruits of them that slept. (1 Cor. 15:20)

When the Lord rose from the grave, He fulfilled the Feast of First Fruits. He is the First Fruits of them that slept, and His resurrection confirmed His victory over sin and death. And ours too, for if you confess with your mouth, "Jesus is Lord," and believe in your heart that God raised Him from the dead; you will be saved (Rom. 10:9).

Since it is often overshadowed by the prominence of Passover, the Feast of First Fruits is pretty much overlooked as a festival event in the New Testament, yet it is mentioned a number of times in the New Covenant. Paul, in his first letter to the believers in Corinth, shows a vital link between First Fruits and the ministry of Jesus: I Cor. 15:20-24 – *"But the fact is that the Messiah has been raised from the dead, the first fruits of those who have died. For since death came through a man, also the resurrection of the dead has come through a man. For just as in connection with Adam all die, so in connection with the Messiah all will be made alive. But each in his own order; the Messiah is the first fruits; then those who belong to the Messiah, at the time of his coming; then the culmination, when he hands over the Kingdom of God to the father after having put an end to every rulership, yes to every authority and power."*

Paul is actually making a technical reference to the holy day of First Fruits. It is not just that Jesus was the first to rise bodily from the grave, but that by so doing, He is the direct fulfillment of the feast of First Fruits. We miss a very important Biblical truth by not using the term "First Fruits" as the name of this feast, because "first" implies a second, third, fourth, and so on, and that is the real meaning of this feast. We are not only celebrating the resurrection of Jesus as First Fruits, we are celebrating the resurrection of the entire body of believers, His Church! We shall all be resurrected and go to heaven, just as the Lord did, "Every man in his own order" (1 Corinthians 15:22,23).

It is very easy to understand God's plan of redemption if we understand the feasts. Jesus was crucified on Passover, placed in the tomb on the Feast of Unleavened Bread and now He celebrates the Feast of First Fruits by rising from the dead and becoming the First Fruits of the dead. Jesus even presented His proper First Fruits offering to our Father on this Feast: *And the graves were opened; and many bodies of the saints which slept arose, and came out of the graves after his resurrection, and went into the holy city, and appeared unto many (Matthew 27:52,53).* Graves were opened and dead people rose and were seen after His resurrection on the streets of Jerusalem. Jesus gratefully offered the Father the wave offering that is the early crops of what will be an overwhelming harvest during the end times. The days of substitutes were over; the real had come. (Hebrews 10:1)

**"He is risen!"**
**"He is risen indeed!"**
*(A Christian Greeting for those in the Underground church in Rome*
*1st – 3rd centuries)*

### *Conclusion*

Like the other spring feasts, this feast found it's fulfillment in the Messiah's first coming. Paul declared this in this seventh and most significant reference to first fruits in the New Testament with this glorious proclamation: *"But now Christ has been raised from the dead, the first fruits of those who are asleep"* (I Cor. 15:20).

It is also our honor and blessing to be considered the first fruits of the work of Christ on earth. James 1:17,18 says: *"Every good thing given and every perfect gift is from above, coming down from the Father of lights, with whom there is no variation or shifting shadow. In the exercise of His will He brought us forth by the word of truth, so that we would be a kind of first fruits among His creatures."* In this regard we are to be useful to the Kingdom of Heaven by spreading the Gospel to the lost, to those whom the Lord has not yet called but will call as the Word of Truth is proclaimed by those of us who are already His followers. Until the Lord returns there will be those who are coming to saving faith and brought into the family of God and we are the Lord's instruments to serve Him in the sharing of the good news. And if we are the first fruits then we can look forward to the joy of seeing other fruit come into the family of God.

## Footnotes for Chapter Four:

1- Robin Sampson, Linda Pierce. *A Family Guide to the Biblical Holidays.* p. 197.
2- The Refiner's Fire. http://www.therefinersfire.org/first_fruits.htm.
3- Robert Boyd. *Exploring Israel's History* . p. 80.
4- Jack Kelly. http://www.gracethrufaith.com.
5- Christ Centered Mall. www.christcenteredmall.com/teachings/feasts/ firstfruits.htm.
6- Alfred Edershiem. *The Temple* . p. 167.
7- Kevin Howard and Marvin Rosenthal. *The Feasts of the Lord* . p. 77.
8- J.T. Barclay. *The City of the Great King* . p. 96.
9- Mishnah. *Menahot (Holy Things)* 8:2. p. 748.
10- The Refiner's Fire. http://www.therefinersfire.org/first_fruits.htm.

## Chapter Five – Perseverance
## Hag Ha-Shavuot - Feast of Pentecost
### *(Fifty Days after The Feast of First Fruits – normally Sivan 6)*

*15 " 'From the day after the Sabbath, the day you brought the sheaf of the wave offering, count off seven full weeks. 16 Count off fifty days up to the day after the seventh Sabbath, and then present an offering of new grain to the LORD. 17 From wherever you live, bring two loaves made of two-tenths of an ephah of fine flour, baked with yeast, as a wave offering of first fruits to the LORD. 18 Present with this bread seven male lambs, each a year old and without defect, one young bull and two rams. They will be a burnt offering to the LORD, together with their grain offerings and drink offerings—an offering made by fire, an aroma pleasing to the LORD. 19 Then sacrifice one male goat for a sin offering and two lambs, each a year old, for a fellowship offering. [ c ] 20 The priest is to wave the two lambs before the LORD as a wave offering, together with the bread of the first fruits. They are a sacred offering to the LORD for the priest. 21 On that same day you are to proclaim a sacred assembly and do no regular work. This is to be a lasting ordinance for the generations to come, wherever you live. 22 " 'When you reap the harvest of your land, do not reap to the very edges of your field or gather the gleanings of your harvest. Leave them for the poor and the alien. I am the LORD your God.' "* (Leviticus 23:15-22)

The Feast of Pentecost also known as The Feast of Weeks, Harvest (Exodus 23:16), Shavuot (Hebrew), or the Day of First Fruits (Numbers 28:26), was a festival of joy and thanksgiving celebrating the completion of the harvest season. The Feast of Pentecost was one of the major holidays of the Old Testament. It was the second feast in which all able-bodied Jewish males were required to attend at the Temple (the other two being Passover and the Feast of Tabernacles). It was celebrated as a Sabbath with rest from ordinary labors and the calling of a holy convocation (Leviticus 23:21; Numbers 28:26).

It is often a hard thing to leave your family, your home, your fields and crops and all your possessions behind and leave for the feast, but we find in Exodus 34:24 that God will protect His people and their possessions during the feasts. *"For I will drive out nations before you and enlarge your borders, and no man shall covet your land when you go up three times a year to appear before the LORD your God.* God did keep His promise and there is no record, Biblical or otherwise, of any attack on Israel ever occurring during one of the three Pilgrim feasts. It is comforting to know that God is looking out for us when we go to worship Him.

Pentecost also marked the receiving of the law of God at Mt. Sinai through the Prophet Moses when the Jewish people were liberated from Egypt and entered into alliance with God nearly fourteen hundred years before Christ's birth. At that time the Jews promised to be obedient to God and He, in turn, promised them His mercy and blessings through salvation by the Messiah who was yet to come. Now because the Feast of Pentecost was first the celebration of the harvest season, it was celebrated with great joy. Many Jews scattered over various parts of the vast Roman Empire hurried to Jerusalem to participate in this feast. Having been born and having grown up in different countries, most of them could hardly understand their mother tongue. They made an effort, however, to observe their national and religious traditions and, at least from time to time, to go on a pilgrimage to Jerusalem **(1).**

### When is the Feast of Pentecost?

Fifty days after the Passover the Israelites accepted a covenant with God. This is the second great historical experience of the Jews as a people – the experience of revelation. Pentecost is the closure of the Passover holiday. On this day, the constitution of the newly liberated people, the Torah, was promulgated (2).

Unlike all the other holidays in the Old Testament, the Feast of Pentecost is not given a fixed calendar date. In fact no date is given for it in the Bible. Instead we are told that it will be celebrated 50 days after the Feast of First Fruits. Normally however, this feast does fall on the 6 th of Sivan.

Essentially a harvest celebration, the term *weeks* was used to describe the time period from the barley harvest to the wheat harvest. It is called the Feast of Weeks because God specifically told the sons of Jacob that they were to count seven sevens of weeks (seven complete weeks) from First fruits (Leviticus 23:15; Deuteronomy 16:9), and then on the "morrow" this fourth feast was to be observed (Luke 23:16). Seven sevens of weeks are forty-nine days. Add one additional day ("on the morrow"), and it brings the total number of days to fifty. This fourth feast was to occur precisely fifty days after First fruits, which was the bringing of the *Omer Offering* in the Temple (and for the Christian was also the time of Christ's resurrection). Therefore, the Feast was also given the name "Pentecost" (Acts 2:1) which means "fifty."

### What Is the Feast of Pentecost?

In the land of Israel both Passover and Pentecost had strong agricultural foundations – Passover linked to the spring and Pentecost to the summer. From Passover to Pentecost, the sowing of the seed in the spring culminates in the summer harvest (3).

There are three Scripture passages that outline the Biblical Feast. The Temple offerings prescribed for this holiday are found in Leviticus 23:15-22 (see above) and Numbers 28:26-31. The requirements of the individual worshippers are set forth in Deuteronomy 16:9-12 (see appendix number six) where they are told to offer a freewill offering, to rejoice before the Lord, and to remember that the Lord had freed them from Egyptian Bondage.

Pentecost is to be a feast in which praise and worship are given to God in thanksgiving for His provisions in the harvest and they are a prayer that God will bless the current harvest to the fullest extent. This feast therefore, is considered to be a solemn feast. It was to be a holy convocation or rest day. No work was to be done on this day (Leviticus 23:21).

Pentecost is basically a time of thanking God for the many blessings that He has given us. God deals righteously with His people. Lets take this time to thank God for his blessings striving always to become the full harvest. Each of the rituals connected to Pentecost contained both thanksgiving and prayers for future blessings. This feast also marked the rite of a new agricultural season. – the bringing of the first fruits of the wheat harvest to the temple (4).

### How was the Feast of Pentecost to be celebrated?

It is interesting to note that the patriarchs kept the Feast of Weeks or Pentecost. The following scripture says that Solomon offered the sacrifices that God required in the law. *Then Solomon offered burnt offerings to God on the altar of God, which he had built before the vestibule, according to the daily rate, offering according to the commandment of Moses, for the Sabbaths, the New Moons, and the three appointed yearly feasts--the Feast of Unleavened Bread, the Feast of Weeks, and the Feast of Tabernacles (2 Chronicles 8:12-13 NKJV).*

On this occasion, the children of Israel were not to simply bring the sheaf of the first fruits of the wheat harvest to the Temple (as they had brought the sheaf of the first fruit of the barley harvest at the Feast of First Fruits), but also two loaves of bread. These two loaves were specifically commanded to be made with fine flour and baked with leaven (Leviticus 23:17). These two loaves had to be made with grain from the current harvest and this grain had to have been grown in Israel (5). These two loaves, together with two lambs, were to be used as a "wave offering" for the people. Then the wave offering was given to the priests and formed the festive meal the priests would eat later in the day in the Temple.

These two loaves, however, could not be eaten until after the ceremony was completed (Leviticus 23:14; Joshua 5:10-11) and could not be placed on the altar due to its leaven content *"No grain offering, which you bring to the LORD, shall be made with leaven, for you shall not offer up in smoke any leaven or any honey as an offering by fire to the LORD"* (Leviticus 2:11). In addition to the wave offering and two lambs, one young bull, and two rams were to be offered as burnt offerings before the Lord (Leviticus 23:15-22; Numbers 28:26-31). The eating of communal meals to which the poor, the stranger, and the Levites were invited concluded the feast **(6).**

The two loaves, which were brought to the Temple, in the Old Testament, represented both Jew and Gentile; however for the New Testament the two loaves became one in Christ with the advent of the Spirit's coming. Writing to the Ephesian believers, Paul said" *"For he is our peace, who hath made both (Jew and Gentile) one, and have broken down the middle wall of partition between us ... to make in himself of two (Jew and Gentile) one new man, so making peace" (Ephesians 2:14-15).* There was to be leaven in those two loaves, for the Church had not yet been glorified. During this age, there is still sin within the Church. The Lord Jesus (the head) is unleavened - that is sinless. On the other hand, the Church (the body) still has leaven (sin) within her. Therefore, leaven was to be included in those two loaves.

The Feast of Pentecost was a time that we are not to appear before the Lord empty. It is a time that we give to God a tribute above and beyond our tithe. (Exodus 23:13-17) It is also a time that even the poor are given a blessing. As we read back Leviticus 23 the corners of the fields were to be left for the poor so that they might also share in the blessing of God. Something important to note here in Exodus 23:13 is that during these times we are not to even mention the names of other deities. *"And in all that I have said to you, be circumspect and make no mention of the name of other deities, nor let it be heard from your mouth" (Ex. 23:13).*

### How is the Feast of Pentecost celebrated in today?

After the Temple was destroyed it was impossible to practice the rituals of this feast and so the rituals were changed. The Sanhedrin convened in 140 AD in the village of Usha near modern day Haifa. They decided to change the meaning of Pentecost. So, instead of dealing with the harvest, the Feast became associated with the giving of God's law to the people at Mt. Sinai (7).

Pentecost therefore came to celebrate the giving of the Torah (Law of God, Ten Commandments), which is the guide for how God's people are to live in this world. The Law is the spelling out of the details of the Covenant that, while initiated by the events of the Exodus, is agreed upon and sealed at Mt.

Sinai. This event is central to the belief and practice of the faith. We must be able to believe in a God who cares about this world and expects us to practice in our lives what is good and just (8). When they made this change in emphasis the Jews became "the people of the book". That is they maintained their identity and distinctiveness through their adherence of the Scriptures laws (9).

In addition, this is the day that the Jewish people remember that God met them at Mount Sinai and they celebrate the fact that this was the time and place of the birth of the Nation of Israel. On this day they also read the book of Ruth because Ruth was a proselyte to Judaism, because of the books reference to the Feast of the Harvest and because of its treatment of strangers and the poor (10).

It is interesting today that people decorate their homes at the Feast of Pentecost with plants and flowers and lots of greenery. The idea is to remember that you belong to the land of Israel (just as the grain for the loaf offerings could only come form the land in Israel) and shows you desire to return to that Promised Land some day (11).

The people call the Feast of Pentecost the greatest feast because one can eat whatever one likes, whenever one likes, wherever one likes. At Passover, leavened breads are forbidden; at the Feast of Tabernacles meals are eaten only in the booths, on the Feast of Trumpets you can only eat after completing lengthy prayers and at Feast of The Day of Atonement you may not eat at all. Since this feasts concerns the giving of the law at Sinai in today's celebrations, there are no food or eating instructions (12).

The Jews today also celebrate the fact that on the Feast of Pentecost in 1967 the Western Wall of the Temple Mount was first open to civilian visitors. An estimated 200,000 Israelis flocked to that spot on that day. Today, tens of thousands of Jews who have stayed up all night studying the Torah walk to the Western Wall at the break of dawn to recite the morning service (13).

For Christians today, this Feast was when Paul was arrested in Jerusalem for taking Greeks into the Temple. He was later sent to Rome for trial. His life was in peril from this moment forward until he died (Acts 20:16). Additionally, many Christians believe that it was at the Feast of Pentecost in Acts that God reversed the punishment of the Tower of Babel of the confusing of the languages. On this day God brought Jews from all parts of the immediate world to the Temple of Jerusalem. On that day the people heard the teaching of the Gospel in their own language, essentially bringing all languages together through the power of the Holy Spirit (14).

## How did God Fulfill the Feast of Pentecost?

The Feast of the Holy Trinity is another name for the Feast of Pentecost and is dedicated to the descent of the Holy Spirit upon the Apostles on the fiftieth day after the Resurrection of Christ. On the feast of Pentecost the Church brings its children to the doors of its spiritual life and appeals to them to renew and strengthen in themselves the gifts of the Holy Spirit given to them in Baptism. Spiritual life in an individual is impossible without God's grace, which possesses the mysterious power of rebirth and transforms the whole of the Christian's inward life. However lofty and valuable his desires might be, they will be only fulfilled in and by the power of the Holy Spirit. That is why the Feast of Pentecost is always so joyfully celebrated by Christians.

Throughout all of history God gradually revealed Himself to mankind even though the Trinity exists and is seen from the very beginning. During Old Testament times people knew only about God the Father. Since the birth of the Savior they learned of his Only-begotten Son, and on the day of the descent of the Holy Spirit people learned of the existence of the Third Person of the Holy Trinity. Thus mankind was instructed to believe and praise God, one in essence and Threefold in Persons, that is, God the Father, and the Son, and the Holy Spirit, the Trinity one and indivisible.

So the Feast of Pentecost is a symbolic festival that points to the coming of the Holy Spirit, introduces the full Trinity and serves as the birthday of the Church. This happened through the work of the Son of God. He arose from the grave on the Feast of First Fruits. He then spent forty days with His disciples in post-resurrection ministry (Acts 1:3). Immediately after forty days, Jesus informed them that it was necessary that He leave them and ascend to His Father in Heaven (in order to apply the benefits of His once and for all sacrifice). However, He told His disciples that they would not be left abandoned and comfortless. He would send them His Holy Spirit as the Comforter who would come alongside to help them experience and live in the salvation He had accomplished for them in His absence and until He comes again (John 14:16-17). The disciples were commanded to tarry at Jerusalem until the Comforter came (Acts 1:4). The disciples waited as they were commanded; however, their wait was not long - only ten days. And then it happened. The Spirit of God descended on those first-century believers " *When the day of Pentecost had come, they were all together in one place. And suddenly a sound came from heaven like the rush of a mighty wind, and it filled all the house where they were sitting. And there appeared to them tongues as of fire, distributed and resting on each one of them" (Acts 2:1-3 RSV).* It is interesting to note here that Jesus' brothers were there and were also filled with the Spirit on this wonderful day. Up until this time we had been told that Jesus brothers did not believe in Him as the Messiah (Acts 1:14).

The Holy Spirit gave each of them the ability to speak and the people from near and far heard the disciples speak in their own language. So when the disciples where discussing the scriptures the multitude was amazed that not only did they hear their own language spoken but they heard the scriptures being spoken. *"And they were all filled with the Holy Spirit and began to speak in other tongues, as the Spirit gave them utterance. Now there were dwelling in Jerusalem Jews, devout men from every nation under heaven. And at this sound the multitude came together, and they were bewildered, because each one heard them speaking in his own language. And they were amazed and wondered, saying, "Are not all these who are speaking Galileans? And how is it that we hear, each of us in his own native language? Parthians and Medes and Elamites and residents of Mesopotamia, Judea and Cappadocia, Pontus and Asia, Phrygia and Pamphylia, Egypt and the parts of Libya belonging to Cyrene, and visitors from Rome, both Jews and proselytes, Cretans and Arabians, we hear them telling in our own tongues the mighty works of Yahweh." And all were amazed and perplexed, saying to one another, "What does this mean?" (Acts 2:4-12 RSV).*

As we see in verse 11 some among the multitude said that they heard the mighty works of God in their own tongues. This is an amazing show of God's power through the Holy Spirit. Then the Apostle Peter, standing with the eleven other apostles, spoke in the Spirit to the crowd. He explained that these strange events had been predicted by the prophet Joel, and that Jesus's coming had been prophesied by David. Peter explained that these events confirmed David's prophesied exaltation of Jesus. Peter then exhorted his listeners to turn to Christ. These people were so impressed that many of them were baptized. Three thousand were baptized that day according to verse 41. About three thousand responded to Peter's sermon.

In his preaching Peter quotes Joel 2:28-32 which says: *"And it shall come to pass afterward that I will pour out My Spirit upon all flesh; and your sons and your daughters shall prophesy, your old men shall dream dreams, your young men shall see visions; and also upon the servants and upon the handmaids in those days will I pour out My Spirit. "And I will show wonders in the heavens and in the earth--blood and fire and pillars of smoke. The sun shall be turned into darkness and the moon into blood, before the great and the terrible day of the Lord shall come. And it shall come to pass, that whosoever shall call on the name of the Lord shall be delivered; for in Mount Zion and in Jerusalem shall be deliverance, as God hath said, and in the remnant whom the Lord shall call.*

Joel speaks in these verses of the last days before the Lord's return. This passage is one of many that point out the importance of calling on God's name. The Lord will deliver them that call on His name. In a generation of Jews that would not use the sacred name this must have been motivating. They were full of the Holy Spirit. Being led by the Spirit many heard them and were pricked in there hearts.

This day represented a change in the way the Holy Spirit was given. David cried to the Lord to not take the Holy Spirit away from him. It is important to realize that before Jesus' sacrifice the Holy Spirit came and left. Now with people that were cleansed through the blood of the Lamb of God the Holy Spirit could stay and help men and women discern the scriptures. Psalms 51:11 *"Do not cast me away from Your presence, And do not take Your Holy Spirit from me.*

Additionally, this day represents a change in the way the Lord reveals His will to His people. In the Old Testament the Lord revealed Himself and His will and His commands to the people through the prophets. During those times when there was no prophet, God revealed His will through the casting of lots. It was the means of decision on the Day of Atonement (Lev. 16:8) and was how the Promised Land had been divided (Joshua 18:10). The people also used the lots after the returned from exile (Nehemiah 10:34; 11:1) and Proverbs 16:33 tells us that the answers we receive from casting the lots are always from the Lord. So there was Biblical and historical precedence for the Apostles to use the lots in the upper room of Acts 1.

But after Acts 1 there are no other Biblical mentions of the casting of lots. Why? Because the Holy Spirit had come. The Holy Spirit is the Spirit of Prophecy that gave the words of God to all the people through the prophets. In times when there was an absence of prophets that Holy Spirit revealed God's will when the lots were cast. But in Acts we see that the Holy Spirit comes to each believer and lives in their heart and gives God's will to them. How does He do this? Through the written Word of God. As we study the Scriptures the Holy Spirit opens our minds, convicts our hearts, guides our actions and soothes our spirits. So, also as we hear the Word preached and as we worship and as we struggle with our sanctification the Holy Spirit reveals to us the will and council of God. In other words, in the Church, since the Book of Acts, God speaks to us through His Holy Spirit.

This Feast of Pentecost also represented a change in who were the people of God. Before the coming of the Holy Spirit Gentiles were considered outsiders, unable to be part of the family of God unless they became proselytes – those who would go through he process of becoming Jewish. Since this day, however, born again believers from all walks of life are now God's chosen people (15). Peter says in I Peter 2:9 " *But you are A Chosen Race, A royal Priesthood, a Holy nation, a people for God's own possession, so that you may*

49

*proclaim the excellencies of Him who has called you out of darkness into His marvelous light."*

### Conclusion

Just as this was the birth of Israel when they received the law at Mt. Sinai, this day in the New Testament is the birth of the church when they received the Holy Spirit. To Christians today the Day of Pentecost is a celebration of a personal relationship with God through His Holy Spirit and the of the giving of the better law *"written not on tablets of stone, but on the fleshy tables of the heart," "with the Spirit of the Living God"* (16). The church, that is the followers of Jesus, is also a harvest of sorts as it represents those people who are believers that are taken out from among men and consecrated to God. The church is a pledge of a fuller harvest that will be gathered in to the Lord in the fullness of time (17).

Finally, to fully understand this Feast of Pentecost we need to also look at the Feast of First Fruits and look at them both in the light of the Lord Jesus. First, in the Feast of First Fruits we have, as the commencement of the new harvest, the Lord Jesus Himself, risen from the dead, the "first fruits" – the first sheaf waved before the Lord on the feast of First Fruits, just as Christ burst the bonds of death with His glorious resurrection at that very time (I Cor. 15:20,23). Then in fulfillment of the Pentecostal type of the first loaves that still contain leaven, we read the outpouring of the Holy Spirit who helps us to work out our sanctification by overcoming sin. Finally in Revelation the scene is transferred to heaven and we see the full application of this symbol of Christ and the Holy Spirit to the church of the firstborn (18). In the words of Paul in Romans 8:23 *"And not only this, but also we ourselves, having the first fruits of the Spirit, even we ourselves groan within ourselves, waiting eagerly for our adoption as sons, the redemption of our body.*

### Footnotes for Chapter Five

1- http://judaism.about.com/library/1_jerusalem/bl_jewishbond_f.htm
2- Irving Greenberg. *The Jewish Way* . p. 26.
3- Ibid.
4- Michael Strassfeld. *The Jewish Holidays, A Guide & Commentary* . p. 69.
5- The Mishna. *Bikkurim* 1.2.C. p. 167
6- David Boshart, Jr. *Weeks.* www.christcenteredmall.com/teachings/feasts/
   weeks.
7- Kevin Howard and Marvin Rosenthal. *The Feasts of the Lord* . p. 94.
8- Michael Strassfeld. *The Jewish Holidays, A Guide & Commentary* . p. 71.
9- Louis Goldberg. *Our Jewish Friends.* P. 49.
10- Ibid.
11- Marguerite Ickis. *The Book of Religious Holidays and Celebrations* . p. 30.
12- Irving Greenberg. *The Jewish Way* . p. 80.
13- Joseph Tulushkin. *Jewish Literacy* . p.593
14- Ernest L. Martin. *The Temples that Jerusalem Forgot* . p. 259.
15- Robert Boyd. *Exploring Israel's History* . p. 189.
16- Alfred Edershiem. *The Temple* . p. 174.
17- Louis Goldberg. *Our Jewish Friends.* P. 50.
18- Alfred Edershiem. *The Temple* . p. 244.

# Interpretation of the Spring Feasts

## *The Feast of Passover - Salvation*

In the Old Testament the people were saved by putting their faith in the Messiah (who we now know was Jesus) that God would send one day. The deliverance that the Messiah would bring from slavery to sin and death was illustrated by the people's deliverance from slavery in Egypt. The symbol of salvation was the blood of the lamb – an animal at the first Passover. In the New Testament people are saved by putting their faith in the Messiah (Jesus) who did come. The symbol of salvation was the blood of the lamb – the Son of God at the last Passover.

After this night – no sacrifices would ever be needed by God again nor would any others ever be accepted. Jesus was the final and perfect sacrifice that was required by God to make all those who would receive Him as their Savior right and holy and pure before the Heavenly Father. Through Jesus sacrifice on the cross and His resurrection, our Heavenly Father kept His promise to us from Genesis 3:15 and made us one with Him in a holy and loving relationship once again and for all eternity.)

## *The Feast of Unleavened Bread - Sanctification*

Leaven came to represent sin. Leaven has to be cleaned out of the house before Passover can be celebrated. So sin must be cleaned out of our hearts before the Lord's Supper can be celebrated. But this cleansing of sin from the heart takes place every day of our lives. As the Israelites took the first steps toward the Promised Land immediately after God saved them from death through the blood of the lamb, so also do we begin the journey of daily sanctification toward eternity in the presence of the Lord immediately after the blood of the Lamb of God, the Lord Jesus is applied to our hearts.

## *The Feast of First Fruits - Adoption*

The harvest cannot be gathered in until the first fruits of the harvest have been sacrificed to God. When the sacrifice is received, God promises to bring in the full harvest and to make it a full and great harvest that will insure the survival of the people for another year. When Jesus rose from the grave He was the first fruit of the spiritual harvest that had been sacrificed and received by God. Because His sacrifice was received God promised to bring in the full harvest of all those who put their faith in Christ alone for salvation and to ensure their place with Him, in His family, for all eternity.

### The Feast of Pentecost - Perseverance

At Mount Sinai God gave the people the law and it was the birth of the Nation of Israel. All those who worked to obey the laws and statutes of God were considered to be a part of the Nation. In Jerusalem at Pentecost in the New Testament times, the Holy Spirit comes and it is the birth of the Church. All those who receive Jesus Christ as their own, personal Lord and Savior are members of the church. Since the Holy Spirit has come, however, He lives in the hearts of the people of God and leads and guides them always to the Father. He preserves His people until the end of time, when Jesus returns.

## Chapter Six – Effectual Calling
## Rosh Hashanah - Feast of Trumpets (Tishri 1)

*...In the seventh month, on the first of the month, there shall be a sabbath for you, a remembrance with shofar blasts, a holy convocation. -* **Leviticus 16:24**

The name "Rosh Hashanah" is not used in the Bible to discuss this holiday. The Bible refers to the holiday as Yom Ha-Zikkaron (the day of remembrance) or Yom Teruah (the day of the sounding of the shofar). The holiday is instituted in Leviticus 23:24-25.

### *Psalm 81 – The Psalm for the New Moon Festival*

*1Sing for joy to God our strength; Shout joyfully to the God of Jacob. 2 Raise a song; strike the timbrel, the sweet sounding lyre with the harp. 3 Blow the trumpet at the new moon, at the full moon, on our feast day. 4 For it is a statute for Israel, An ordinance of the God of Jacob. 5 He established it for a testimony in Joseph when he went throughout the land of Egypt.*

*I heard a language that I did not know: 6 "I relieved his shoulder of the burden, his hands were freed from the basket. 7"You called in trouble and I rescued you; I answered you in the hiding place of thunder; I proved you at the waters of Meribah. Selah.*

*8"Hear, O My people, and I will admonish you; O Israel, if you would listen to Me! 9"Let there be no strange god among you; nor shall you worship any foreign god. 10"I, the LORD, am your God, who brought you up from the land of Egypt; Open your mouth wide and I will fill it. 11"But My people did not listen to My voice, And Israel did not obey Me. 12"So I gave them over to the stubbornness of their heart, to walk in their own devices.*

*13"Oh that My people would listen to Me, that Israel would walk in My ways! 14"I would quickly subdue their enemies and turn My hand against their adversaries. 15"Those who hate the LORD would pretend obedience to Him, and their time of punishment would be forever. 16"But I would feed you with the finest of the wheat, and with honey from the rock I would satisfy you."*

### *The Festivals of Israel*

*The LORD said to Moses, "Say to the Israelites: 'On the first day of the seventh month you are to have a day of rest, a sacred assembly commemorated with trumpet blasts. Do no regular work, but present an offering made to the LORD by fire.' " (Leviticus 23:23-25)*

*The LORD spoke further to Moses, saying, "Make yourself two trumpets of silver, of hammered work you shall make them; and you shall use them for summoning the congregation and for having the camps set out. "When both are blown, all the congregation shall gather themselves to you at the doorway of the tent of meeting. "Yet if only one is blown, then the leaders, the heads of the divisions of Israel, shall assemble before you...*"When convening the assembly, however, you shall blow without sounding an alarm. "The priestly sons of Aaron, moreover, shall blow the trumpets; and this shall be for you a perpetual statute throughout your generations...*"Also in the day of your gladness and in your appointed feasts, and on the first days of your months, you shall blow the trumpets over your burnt offerings, and over the sacrifices of your peace offerings; and they shall be as a reminder of you before your God. I am the LORD your God." (Numbers 10:1-10)*

*"Now in the seventh month, on the first day of the month, you shall also have a holy convocation; you shall do no laborious work. It will be to you a day for blowing trumpets." (Numbers 29:1)*

Rosh Hashanah or Jewish New Year is called the Feast of Trumpets in the Bible because it begins the Jewish High Holy Days and Ten Days of Repentance with the blowing of the ram's horn, the shofar, calling God's people together to repent from their sins. During Rosh Hashanah synagogue services, the trumpet traditionally sounds 100 notes. Rosh Hashanah is also the start of the civil year in Israel. It is a solemn day of soul-searching, forgiveness, repentance and remembering God's judgment, as well as a joyful day of celebration, looking forward to God's goodness and mercy in the New Year. Rosh Hashanah is celebrated on the first day of the Hebrew month of Tishri (September or October).

The Feast of Trumpets, celebrated on the first day of the seventh month (Tishri), marked the end of the agricultural year. The seventh month is an important month because it also included two major holy days – the Day of Atonement and the Feast of Booths. It has some other important meanings as well, which we will discuss further in this chapter. The long and loud blowing of trumpets always announced the commencement of this special month.

Rosh Hashanah literally means "Head of the Year" and this feast is the second New Year of the Jewish people. The Feast of Passover is their Religious New Year and the Feast of Trumpets is the Civil New Year. It was also called the memorial of the "Blowing of Trumpets" and the "Day of Blowing of Trumpets." The New Year emphasis, although always a theme of the Feast of Trumpets, really came into prominence as part of the celebration after the destruction of the Temple in 70 AD **(1).**

This feast is the first of the Fall Feasts of Israel and combined with the Day of Atonement and the Days of Awe is considered part of the *High Holy Days*. In connection with these days, one of the major themes of this feast is repentance, judgment and atonement. Even though this is a one-day feast, it is actually the beginning of a season of repentance culminating in the Day of Atonement. It emphasizes a striving for atonement of our sins of the past year and longs for forgiveness and salvation (2). The focus of forgiveness in this feast however, is on God's willingness to give us forgiveness out of his own goodness and love for us. *"Good and upright is the LORD; Therefore He instructs sinners in the way" (Psalm 25:8). "Return to Him from whom you have deeply defected, O sons of Israel" (Isaiah 31:6). "Return, O faithless sons, I will heal your faithlessness. Behold, we come to You For You are the LORD our God" (Jeremiah 3:22).*

In ancient Israel the new moons were normally announced by short blasts of the trumpet, but the new moon of the seventh month was celebrated by long blasts, emphasizing its solemnity and uniqueness among months (3). One of the horns blown at this feast was made from a ram's horn, and was called the "shofar," as we can see in Psalm 81 above, and the blowing of this horn pointed to the ram that God had provided when Abraham offered Isaac as a sacrifice to the Lord. God provided the ram instead of Isaac, to show that salvation was the gift of God and that man could not atone for his own sins. In fact the shofar's call is a reminder to the people that God is sovereign *"God has ascended with a shout, the Lord with the sound of the trumpet!" (Psalm 47:5)*

### *When is the Feast of Trumpets?*

This holiday and its emphasis on repentance is considered to be so important to God's people that they begin preparing for it a whole month early in the sixth month of Elul. According to Jewish tradition Moses went up Mt. Sinai for the second time to receive the tables of the law again and remained there for forty days. Then he descended to the waiting and forgiven people on the Day of Atonement. Since then the days of Elul have been consecrated as days of repentance as they lead into the Feast of Trumpets (4). So even though the Feast of Tabernacles begins on Tishri 1, preparation for it begins a whole month earlier. Every day of this month the shofar is blown to remind the people that Rosh Hashanah, the Day of Judgment is coming.

This is the only feast, which occurs on the first day of the month at the new moon, when the moon is dark and only a thin crescent and is in the autumn of the year. In the Scriptures this is a one day holiday but after the destruction of Israel this became a two day holiday. This was because of the difficulty in establishing the first day of the new moon, which was the actual date of the holiday, for every Jewish community that wanted to celebrate the feast wherever they were in the world. To make sure there were no mistakes or any community of the Diaspora left out, it was extended for two days.

In Israel seven is a holy number. Both the seventh day of the week and the seventh year were holy under the Mosaic Law (Exodus 29:8-10; Leviticus 25:4). So also Tishri, the seventh month was holy to the people. This month is considered the Sabbath month of the year and the Feast of Trumpets occurs on the first day of this month in which all the fall feasts of Israel occur.

### What Is the Feast of Trumpets?

As already stated, the Feast of the Trumpets is the Jewish Civil New Year, and it is the beginning of the Days of Awe (the days of repentance), however it is also has other aspects to its celebration. One of these is that it is a day to remember the great events of God in the history of His people. In the Torah this Feast Day is called the "Day of Remembering" as the Rabbis call the people to remember the mighty works of God.

The ancient Rabbis believed that God began Creation (3760 BC) on the first day of the seventh month (the Sabbath month – Tishri). They also believed that the first sin (the fall into sin) and repentance took place on this day in 3760 BC. Additionally the Rabbis taught that Noah released the dove for the third time on this day in 2105 BC, that Isaac was bound by Abraham to be a sacrifice in 1677 BC and that on the day of Isaac's binding, his mother, Sarah, passed away at age 127, and was subsequently buried in the Machpelah Cave in Hebron (5).

On this day, after the Jews had returned from the Babylonian captivity, Ezra 3:5 says that the high altar was restored and the people began sacrificing on it. In Nehemiah 8:1-2, the Old Testament Law was read to them and they were so overcome with grief at having neglected God and the sabbatical years so long; they broke down and cried in repentance. Ezra, the prophet, comforted them and reminded them that this festival time was a time of rejoicing and thanksgiving to the Lord (Nehemiah 8:10).

This feast day was also used to speak of God's displeasure with the people. Perhaps because there were extra sacrifices on this day or perhaps because it represented the Sabbath and the worship of God both as the Sabbath month and in regard to the weekly Sabbath. But when the Lord is angry with the people he frequently condemns their "New Moon" sacrifices, including the Feast of Trumpets new moon. We see this in Isaiah 1:13-14; Amos 8:5 and a statement of the unimportance of new moon festivals in Colossians 2:16 (6).

Another aspect of this holiday that we have mentioned earlier is the sounding or blowing of horns. God used the sounding of the trumpet in various ways with Israel (see Numbers 10 above). On this feast it was used to call the people to repentance, to awaken them from sin. It was used to remind them of the covenants God had with His people, which showed His mercy and grace toward them. The blowing of the horn on New Year's Day was to remind the people of their shortcomings and sin and call them to repentance.

The trumpet was actually also the signal for the field workers to come into the Temple. The high priest stood on the southwestern parapet of the Temple and blew the trumpet so it could be heard in the surrounding fields. The Old Testament saints who faithfully followed the Lord would immediately stop the harvest even if it was not finished and leave for the Temple to worship God (7).

### What is the Meaning of the Feast of Trumpets?

Rosh Hashanah is a day of repentance, because the Day of Atonement (Yom Kippur) follows ten days later. Israel was called to repent of their sin and make ready for the Day of Atonement when the High Priest would enter the Holy of Holies in the Tabernacle and later the Temple and sprinkle the blood of a lamb on the Mercy Seat which is atop the Ark of the Covenant between to the two Cherubim.

There were also prescribed sacrifices that had to be given and Numbers 28:11-15 record the sacrifices offered to the Lord on this feast. *"...you shall present a burnt offering to the LORD: two bulls and one ram, seven male lambs one year old without defect; and three-tenths of an ephah of fine flour mixed with oil for a grain offering, for each bull; and two-tenths of fine flour mixed with oil for a grain offering, for the one ram; and a tenth of an ephah of fine flour mixed with oil for a grain offering for each lamb, for a burnt offering of a soothing aroma, an offering by fire to the LORD. Their drink offerings shall be half a hin of wine for a bull and a third of a hin for the ram and a fourth of a hin for a lamb; this is the burnt offering of each month throughout the months of the year. And one male goat for a sin offering to the LORD; it shall be offered with its drink offering in addition to the continual burnt offering."* We must remember though, that these sacrifices were not to actually atone for sin, but were offered in faith, looking to the future when the Messiah, would come and take away the sins of the world (Isaiah 53).

The Feast of Trumpets was also the time of testimony to the Kingship of God over the lives of the people. The blowing of the trumpets was a symbolic confession and proclamation of the Lord as "Jehovah their God" which brought the people before God to be remembered and saved (8).

### *How was the Feast of Trumpets to be celebrated?*

On the first day of every month trumpets were blown and special sacrifices were given to remind the people monthly of their need to live their lives faithfully for their God and King! The same thing happened on this Feast Day but the trumpets were blown louder and longer and more fuller in trumpet blasts. It was also a fuller day because of the amount of sacrifices. This day was considered to be a Holy Convocation to God or a Sabbath and no "servile work" was to be done.

Typically the Feast of Trumpets was celebrated in the local synagogues and not in Jerusalem at the Temple alone. Though we do not have a total picture presented in Scripture and Jewish tradition, the order of the day went something like this:
- The Council sat from early morning to just before the Evening, to determine the appearance of the new moon.
- The proclamation of the Council "It is sanctified!" and not the actual appearance of the new moon, determined the commencement of the feast.
- Immediately afterwards the priests blew the trumpets which marked the feast. These trumpets were blown all day long. Because of this Numbers 29:1 calls this the "Day of Blowing". The mouthpieces for the fast days blowing of trumpets were silver, but the mouthpiece for the Feast of Trumpets was gold.
- After the ordinary morning sacrifices, the prescribed festive offerings were brought, the blood of the burnt offerings being thrown around the base of the altar, and the rest poured out onto the channel at the south side of the altar; while the blood of the sin offering was sprinkled or dropped from the finger on the horns of the altar of burnt offering, beginning from the east, the rest being poured out as that of the burnt offering.
- 107 priests officiated at this sacrifice. 20 with each bullock, 11 with each ram and 8 with every lamb.
- This included those who carried the appropriate food and drink for offerings. While the drink offering was being poured out, the Priests and Levites chanted Psalm 81.
- At the offering of these sacrifices the trumpets were again blown.
- All day special prayers were recited before the Lord. However, none of these prayers have survived from the days of the Temple (9).

This feast was a very popular feast because families could give and celebrate their special annual sacrifice like David did in I Samuel 20. It was also popular because it was a feast day in which those who sought for instruction and edification conducted religious meetings like Elisha did in 2 Kings 4:23 (10).

Later both Isaiah and Ezekiel would teach that this feast has a higher purpose and meaning. There would come a time, according to Isaiah, when the New Moon Trumpet would summon, "all flesh to worship before God" (Isaiah 66:23). Isaiah envisioned the day when the shofar blast would announce the gathering of dispersed Israel (Isaiah 27:13). And according to Ezekiel the closed Eastern Gate to the inner courts of the new Temple will be opened once more to believing Israel on this day (Ezekiel 46:1).

Watchfulness was also a critical ingredient of this feast. It was required that at least two witnesses would see the crescent moon. They would then go to the Council in the Temple and report what they had seen. The High Priest would confirm the sighting and then, as mentioned above, the Council would sit for the day and make the determination on when the feast began.

All of this procedure is both because of excitement over the feast and in terms of accuracy over when the feast was to start. As already stated, the feast begins at the new moon when only the crescent is visible (actually when the Council declares it as seen earlier). This not only determines the new moon of this month but also determines the beginning of the yearly lunar cycle.

This need for watchfulness and preparedness is echoed in the New Testament in connection with the Lord's second coming: II Timothy 2:13 says *"Watching for that blessed hope, and the glorious appearing of the great God and our Savior, Jesus Christ."*

### How did Jesus Fulfill the Feast of Trumpets?

The primary picture of this Feast is repentance and preparation for atonement. On the Feast of Trumpets we begin a ten-day period of repentance as we look forward to the Day of Atonement. We examine our hearts at the prompting and leading of the Holy Spirit. Then we confess our sins and repent over them. Then we receive salvation through faith on the Day of Atonement.

In the Old Testament this faith was in the annual sacrifice on Yom Kippur when the High Priest put the blood on the Ark of the Covenant. When the High Priest left the Holy of Holies alive, it was a testimony that God had accepted the sacrifice and our sins of the past year were forgiven. Since Jesus the Messiah has come this faith is in Him as the final and perfect sacrifice - the Lamb of God who shed His blood to take away our sins. So the Feast of Trumpets focuses on repentance leading to salvation through faith in Jesus Christ.

Rabbi Eliezer, one of Israel's ancient Rabbis, declared, "Repent one day before your death." His astonished disciples asked, "Does then one know on what day he will die?" The Rabbi replied, "Then all the more reason that he repent today (11)." The idea of course is that men do not know when they are going to die and so today is the day of repentance. So to celebrate this feast we are reminded of our need for repentance before the Lord Jesus as 1 John 1:9 says , *"If we confess our sins, He is faithful and righteous to forgive us our sins and to cleanse us from all unrighteousness."*

Rosh Hashanah is also known as the Day of Judgment. At the Final Judgment spoken of in Revelation 20:15, we read that "anyone whose name was not found recorded in the Book of Life was thrown into the lake of fire." The book of Revelation also speaks of this Book of Life as belonging to the Lamb , Jesus Christ (Revelation 21:27).

The New Testament reveals in John 5:27 that the Father has given his Son, Jesus, authority to judge everyone, and 2 Timothy 4:1 says that Jesus will judge the living and the dead. Jesus told his followers in John 5:24, *"I tell you the truth, those who listen to my message and believe in God who sent me have eternal life. They will never be condemned for their sins, but they have already passed from death into life."* Therefore, through our acceptance of his sacrifice and atonement for sin, Jesus has become the fulfillment of this Old Testament feast so closely associated with repentance and judgment.

### *Prophetic Fulfillment*
### *"Blessed assurance, Jesus is mine! Oh what a foretaste of glory divine!"*

The concept of repentance is far more basic to God's word than prophecy. However, Christians characterize the new Moon Festivals as shadows of things that were to come with the reality being found in Christ. So prophecy is an aspect of how Jesus will fulfill this Feast at a future date.

The themes of God as King (in the New Testament Jesus Christ as King) and Feast of Trumpets as the birthday of the world are intertwined with those using this as a period of repentance because God is in the process of judging all living things. We see these themes fulfilled in Christ as the King who has been given all authority to judge the living and the dead by God our Father.

In Middle Eastern cultures and societies the coronation of Kings *usually* took place in the fall. To celebrate the Kingship of God as King above all Kings was an integral part of this feast as a testimony to the people and to the nations. One of the customs of Israel was to blow the trumpets whenever a new

King was ordained and whenever the King arrived. The Shofar was blown everywhere the King went to proclaim his majesty.

So, at the last day, the trumpets will be blown to announce God's Kingship: *With trumpets and sound of cornet [shofar] make a joyful noise before the LORD, the King (Ps. 98:6).* The blowing of the trumpets will announce the coming of the King of the Universe. The Feast of Trumpets & blowing of trumpets symbolizes the Kingship of Christ and His Second Coming. *"Behold, I shew you a mystery; we shall not all sleep, but we shall all be changed, in a moment, in the twinkling of an eye, at the last trump: for the trumpet shall sound, and the dead shall be raised incorruptible, and we shall be changed" (1 Corinthians 15:51-52).*

As mention above in this section, this day will also be a day of judgment. The Feast of Trumpets begins when the sky is darkest and the moon is at its smallest appearance of light. This is symbolic of that great, dark and terrible Day of the Lord when the Lord will pour out His fiery judgment on Israel as well as on her enemies. The prophet Amos says that the Day of the Lord is a "day of darkness and not a day of light" (Amos 5:18-20). The prophet Zephaniah says in 1:14-16: *"Near is the great day of the LORD, Near and coming very quickly; Listen, the day of the LORD! In it the warrior cries out bitterly. A day of wrath is that day, A day of trouble and distress, a day of destruction and desolation, a day of darkness and gloom, a day of clouds and thick darkness, a day of trumpet and battle cry..."* Even as the darkening of the moon in the night heavens announced the Feast of Trumpets, so too, the heavens will be divinely darkened in a future day as the Day of the Lord commences (12). The Apostle John also mentions the darkness which will accompany the Day of the Lord in Revelation 6:12-17.

So this Feast Day, which is centered for the most part on repentance and preparation for atonement from the Lord, does have those Scriptures, which give it a future redemptive aspect as well. Another example is when the Scriptures speak of men or angels blowing trumpets. The Scriptures mention this frequently yet only twice is it recorded that God blows a trumpet. In both instances it is the shofar that is blown and which came to represent the Feast of Trumpets. The first time God blows the shofar is in Exodus 19:18-20 when God descends on Mt. Sinai to speak with Moses. The Lord descended to Mt. Sinai with *"fire, smoke and the blast of the shofar."* He meets with Moses and gives them what they need to have a relationship with Him until the Messiah comes and restores us to God permanently.

The Messiah has come, salvation has been accomplished and is being applied according to His perfect will and plan and He reigns in heaven until the day of His return. It is when our Savior returns that we will experience the second time God blows the shofar. We are told about this future blowing of the shofar in Zechariah, Jeremiah, Ezekiel and I Corinthians. Zechariah 9:14 says: *Then the LORD will appear over them, and His arrow will go forth like lightning; And the Lord GOD will blow the trumpet, and will march in the storm winds of the south.* The last trump will announce the coming and coronation of the Messiah, for He alone will be exalted in that day (Isaiah 2:17).

As the Day of the Lord begins, God's last trump will be sounded, the Messiah will reveal Himself, and He will bring about the end of time through His righteous judgment. *"Behold, days are coming,"* declares the LORD, *"when I will make a new covenant with the house of Israel and with the house of Judah"* (Jeremiah 31:31; see also Ezekiel 20:35-38 and (Zechariah 13:9). *"Behold, I shew you a mystery; we shall not all sleep, but we shall all be changed, in a moment, in the twinkling of an eye, at the last trump: for the trumpet shall sound, and the dead shall be raised incorruptible, and we shall be changed"* (1 Corinthians 15:51-52). According to ancient Jewish tradition, the resurrection of the dead will occur on the Feast of Trumpets. Reflecting this tradition, Jewish gravestones were often engraved with a shofar.

### *Conclusion*

In the spring feasts we saw the picture of God's salvation for His people. In the fall feasts we see more how that salvation is applied. Passover reveals our justification, Unleavened Bread reveals our sanctification, First Fruits reveals our adoption and Pentecost shows our perseverance in salvation. Here in Feast of Trumpets we see that salvation comes through repentance of sins and atonement given to us by a sovereign God. This atonement will have future fulfillment in perfection for all eternity. The other fall feasts also speak to the means of our salvation.

**Footnotes for Chapter Six:**

1- Judaism 101. http://www.jewfaq.org/holiday2.htm.
2- Michael Strassfeld. *The Jewish Holidays, A Guide & Commentary* . p. 95.
3- Kevin Howard and Marvin Rosenthal. *The Feasts of the Lord* . p. 105.
4-Mitch and Zhava Glaser. *The Fall Feasts of Israel* . p. 44.
5- Chabad.org. Calendar. www.chabad.org/calendar/view/day.asp?
    tDate=9/13/2007.
6- James Hastings. *A Dictionary of the Bible, A – Feasts* . P. 859 & 863.
7- Bible Truth Web site. *The Jewish Feasts* . http://www.bible-truth.org/
    Feasts- Trumpets.html.
8-Alfred Edershiem. *The Temple* . p. 191.
9- Ibid, p.192.
10- Ibid, p. 151.
11- Mishnah. *Shabbat 153a* . p. 179.
12- Kevin Howard and Marvin Rosenthal. *The Feasts of the Lord* . p. 113.

# Chapter Seven – Confession and Repentance
## Yomim Noraim - Days of Awe
## (Tishri 1-10)

*It is a Day of Atonement, to make atonement for you before the Lord your God. For whatsoever soul it be that shall not be afflicted in that same day, he shall be cut off from his people. And whatsoever soul it be that doeth any manner of work in that same day, that soul will I destroy from among his people. Ye shall do no manner of work; it is a statute forever throughout your generations in all your dwellings. It shall be a Sabbath of solemn rest, and ye shall afflict your souls "* (Leviticus 23:28b-32).

*For it is written, As I live, saith the Lord, every knee shall bow to me, and every tongue shall confess to God. - Romans 14:11*

"One day -every knee shall bow before God" - Jewish Talmud

"On Rosh Hashanah it is written, and on Yom Kippur it is sealed, how many shall leave this world, and how many shall be born into it, who shall live and who shall die, who shall live out the limit of his days and who shall not, who shall perish by fire and who by water... who shall be at peace and who shall be tormented.... But penitence, prayer, and good deeds can annul the severity of the decree.' -- *Rosh Hashanah Liturgy (1)*

The emphasis on Rosh Hashanah is the Kingship of God, often declared in prayer as "Our Father, Our King." The shofar is blown numerous times during the services, calling upon Jews to remember the sacrifice of Isaac and asking God to impute his righteousness to them. The service concludes with the plea, *"May our names be inscribed into the Book of Life."* The following days are the days of Teshuvah (repentance), where synagogue attendance increases and good deeds are performed. These are the *Days of Awe.*

The Days of Awe are not an actual Feast of Israel, but they are part of the festival program. They connect Rosh Hashanah and Yom Kippur with a time of repentance and spiritual reflection. These three special seasons, together with Elul, the month of preparation preceding Rosh Hashanah, make up the High Holy Days – 40 days of Repentance **(2).**

### When are the Days of Awe?

The Days of Awe are ten days that begin with Rosh Hashanah, the festival that is such a delicate balance between the Jew's eternal confidence in God's mercy and his fear that the inadequacy of his deeds makes him fall short

65

of the minimum threshold of performance (3). These ten days are also known as the Days of Repentance and end with Yom Kippur, the festival of atonement and salvation. This is a time for serious introspection, a time to consider the sins of the previous year before Yom Kippur's sacrifice occurs. This important period, which always occurs in the autumn (the month of Tishri), focuses on repentance, and atonement for sin. These days are called the terrible or dreadful days because of the great solemnity and uncertainty of judgment. At the end of these days people greet one another with "May the final verdict be favorable (4)."

## *What Are the Days of Awe?*

The Days of Awe are called in Hebrew "Yameem Nora-eem". The root word of nora-eem is the Hebrew word "yare". Yare means to be afraid, to fear, to revere, to have a positive feeling of reverence for God. We see the word used in Genesis 3:10 *"And he [Adam] said, "I heard the sound of Thee in the garden, and I was afraid because I was naked; so I hid myself."* These ten Days of Awe are ten days of fearing God.

A parallel word to yare is "guwr". It can mean to stand in awe, to be in awe, to be afraid, to dread, to fear. But it can also mean to sojourn, to dwell, to remain, to inhabit, to abide. *Let all the earth fear the LORD; Let all the inhabitants of the world stand in awe of Him. Ps.33:8. I am the vine, you are the branches; he who abides in Me, and I in him, he bears much fruit; for apart from Me you can do nothing." - John 15:5.* These positive expressions of the Days of Awe are what give hope as we approach Yom Kippur – the Day of Atonement. In addition to being the ten days of fearing God, these are also known as the days of forgiveness.

From the combined themes of fear, dwell, abide, death, forgiveness and judgment comes the central image underlying the Days of Awe: the trial. The Jews envision a trial in which the individual stands before the one who knows all. One's life is placed on the balance scales. A thorough assessment is made: "Is my life contributing to the balance of life? Or does the net effect of my actions tilt the scale toward death? My life is being weighed; I am on trial for my life. Who shall live and who shall die (5)?"

But later the Day of Atonement occurs and sins *can* be forgiven and we *can* be right with God again. This is why the tone of the Days of Awe is basically hopeful, even joyful. This is why the liturgy bursts with life. "Remember us for life, King who loves life; write us in the book of life, for your sake, Lord of Life" (6).

For the Jews, these days are a mixture of works and grace, of repentance and forgiveness, of charity and synagogue attendance. They examine themselves to see if their good works and faithful obedience to the law have been enough to earn God's favor, forgiveness of sin and heaven. But they are also looking to the Day of Atonement and God's grace. The day when they pray that a loving God will accept them and love them and forgive their sins.

"The Days of Awe are filled with reflection and solemnity. The Bible presents a truth about the need for a broken spirit and a contrite heart. Judaism accepts this view and vividly paints the picture that can teach all of us to humbly approach God. Being broken before God is more than the key to humility. It is a very special language that the God of Israel understands and hears with compassion. He desires to listen often and carefully to His repentant children (7)".

### *What is the Meaning of the Days of Awe?*

God's sovereignty in both judgment and repentance and salvation is the overwhelming theme of the Days of Awe. According to the Rabbis man is born with an evil inclination, of which repentance is the anti-dote. Repentance is more than just turning form sin; it is also a return to God and to the right path. The desire of God is that all repent and not face the penalty for sin **(8)**.

The framework of these days is the concept that God has three "books" that he writes our names in, writing down who will live and who will die, who will have a good life and who will have a bad life, for the next year. The first book is the Book of the Righteous and in it are the names of all those who have returned to God. Everybody else is divided into two groups. The first group is the wholly wicked and their names are entered into the Book of the Wicked. Their fate is sealed forever on Rosh Hashanah for they have forever rejected, of their own accord, the salvation that God provided through His Messiah (9).

The last group is written in the Book of the Intermediaries. This is the largest group and is made up of the common people. They are not yet in the Book of the Righteous or the Wicked. They are given 10 more days by God to repent. If they repent before the Day of Atonement their names are moved to the Book of the Righteous. If not, they are moved to the Book of the Wicked. Either way their fate is sealed on the Day of Atonement. (10).

So while these books are written in on Rosh Hashanah, our actions during the Days of Awe can alter God's decree. The actions that change the decree are "teshuvah, tefilah and tzedakah," repentance, prayer, and good deeds (usually, charity). These "books" are finally sealed on Yom Kippur. This concept of writing in books is the source for another one of the common greetings during this time is "May you be inscribed and sealed for a good year (11)."

As just mentioned, while judgment on each person is pronounced on Rosh Hashanah, it is not made absolute until Yom Kippur. The Ten Days of Awe are therefore an opportunity to mend one's ways in order to alter the judgment in one's favor. So for the Jews, the Days of Awe are a time of repentance with the motivation of changing God's mind and feelings toward them. People are confronted with their sins, failings and shortcomings and are more willing and even eager to seek healing with God before the Day of Judgment. While the Scriptures say *"Seek the Lord while He may be found."* (Isaiah 55:6) the Rabbis taught when the Lord could be found specifically. Rabbi bar Abuha said: "He may be found during the ten days between Rosh Hashanah and Yom Kippur (12)."

### How were the Days of Awe to be celebrated?

Among the customs of this time, is the predominate tradition that this is a time to seek reconciliation with people you may have wronged during the course of the year. The Torah has two different sacrifices for dealing with sins. The first is known as the sin offering and the other is known as the guilt offering. The sin offering is for making restitution with God when we sin against Him. The guilt offering is for making restitution with man when we sin against them. Forgiveness for sinning against another person would not be given to you by God until you had first made restitution with the person you had sinned against (13). Thus the Talmud maintains that Yom Kippur atones only for sins between man and God. To atone for sins against another person, you must first seek reconciliation with that person, righting the wrongs you committed against them if possible (14).

So during these days of penitence between these two solemn assemblies, observant Jews think about their sins and go to one another seeking forgiveness. There is a sense in which Jews understand the need to forgive one another if they are to find forgiveness. Certainly, this belief is one of many, which the early Church imported into the faith of our forefathers.

The Ten Days of Awe or Repentance include the Fast of Gedaliah, on the third day of Tishri, and Shabbat Shuvah, which is the Sabbath between Rosh Hashanah and Yom Kippur. Shabbat Shuvah has a special reading from the prophets and traditionally the Rabbis give a long sermon on that day.

The Feast of Gedaliah is a fast day lamenting the expulsion from Israel. The fast begins at first morning light. It commemorates the assassination of Gedaliah Ben Achikam, and the true start of Babylonian exile of the Jewish people (early 6th century B.C.). The Feast of Gedaliah is when the Babylonian King Nebuchadnezzar conquered Jerusalem. He deported the poor inhabitants and left a simple man, Gedaliah, son of Achikam, in charge of the now-Babylonian province. Many Jews who had fled to Moab, Ammon, Edom, and other neighboring lands returned to the land of Judah, tended the vineyards given to them by the king of Babylonia, and enjoyed a new respite after their earlier oppression.

The King of Ammon, however, hostile and envious of the Judean remnant, sent a Jew, Yishmael Ben Netaniah, to assassinate Gedaliah. In the seventh month, Ishmael came to Gedaliah in the town of Mitzpa, and was received cordially. Gedaliah had been warned of his guest's murderous intent, but refused to believe his informants, having the belief that their report was mere slander. Ishmael murdered Gedaliah, together with most of the Jews who had joined him and many Babylonians whom the Babylonian King had left with Gedaliah. The remaining Jews feared the vengeance of the Babylonian King (seeing as his chosen ruler, Gedaliah, had been killed by a Jew) and fled to Egypt. The events are recounted in the Bible. *"But it came to pass in the seventh month, that Ishmael the son of Nethaniah, the son of Elishama, of the seed royal, came, and ten men with him, and smote Gedaliah, that he died, and the Jews and the Chaldeans that were with him at Mizpah. And all the people, both small and great, and the captains of the forces, arose, and came to Egypt; for they were afraid of the Chaldeans."* 2 Kings 25:25-26

The surviving remnant of Jews was thus dispersed and the land remained desolate. In remembrance of these tribulations, Jewish sages instituted the 'Fast of the Seventh' (see Zechariah 8:19) on the day of Gedaliah's assassination in the seventh month. There is some suggestion that Gedaliah was slain on the first day of Tishri, but the fast was postponed till after Rosh Hashanah, since fasting is prohibited during a festival.

Concerning this fast day, the Rabbis have said that its aim is to establish that the death of the righteous is likened to the burning of the house of God. Just as they ordained a fast upon the destruction of the Jewish Temple, likewise they ordained a fast upon the death of Gedaliah.

Another custom for these days is when on the afternoon of the first day of this period it is customary for the Jewish people to perform a rite known as *Tashlik*. To do this, they usually walk to a river, spring or body of water and recite special penitential prayers and Psalms, while at the same time emptying their pockets and the hems of their garments, or casting breadcrumbs onto the water. All this is symbolic of casting away their sins into the deep (Micah 7:18-20) **(15).**

Another custom observed during this time is Kapparot. This is rarely practiced today, and is observed in its true form only by Chasidic and occasionally Orthodox Jews. Basically, you purchase a live fowl, and on the morning before Yom Kippur you wave it over your head reciting a prayer asking that the fowl be considered atonement for sins. The fowl is then slaughtered and given to the poor (or its value is given). Some Jews today simply use a bag of money instead of a fowl. Most Reform and Conservative Jews have never even heard of this practice **(16)**.

Work is permitted as usual during the intermediate Days of Awe, from Tishri 3 to Tishri 9, except of course for Shabbat during that week. The Shabbat (Sabbath) that occurs in this period is known as Shabbat Shuvah (the Sabbath of Return) and is considered to be a rather important Shabbat. It is called the Shabbat of Return because its special reading from the prophet Hosea which begins with the words "Shuvah Yisrael" "Return O Israel". It is also referred to as Shabbat Shuvah because it falls during the Ten Days of Awe or Repentance and is considered to be part of the High Holy Days **(17)**. The Jews believed that this Shabbat was given to Israel as a time for Torah study and prayer. And although one should always take care not to pass the time idly or in inappropriate conversation, on Shabbat Shuvah one should be especially careful to concentrate entirely on the Torah, prayer, and reflection on repentance . You will thereby attain forgiveness for whatever unfitting behavior may have marred other Sabbaths.

Today the *Un'saneh Tokef* is generally recited during our Days of Awe. This famous prayer was developed during the Christian persecution of Jews during the Crusades. This poetic prayer speaks of the sanctity of God's Day of Judgment. We read, "The great shofar is sounded. A still, small voice is heard. This day even angels are alarmed, seized with fear and trembling as they declare: 'the Day of Judgment is here!'" Then a mournful dirge is sung: "*B'Rosh Hashanah, yi-ka-say-vun, yi-ka-say-vun, uv yom tzom kippur yay-cha-say-moon, yay-cha-say-moon.* " The translation is as follows: "On Rosh Hashanah it is written and on Yom Kippur it is sealed." This is why Jews fast and afflict their souls on *Yom Kippur*. They beat their breasts and cry out for forgiveness **(18)**.

Finally, on the last day of the Days of Awe – the evening before Yom Kippur the Day of Atonement we hear the *Kol Nidrei* prayer chanted. It is intoned with a solemn melody and the intensity of the moment echoes in the soul. This famous prayer is actually an Aramaic legal formula that annuls all unresolved vows that were made during the year. It is a protection against rash or coerced oaths that cannot or should not be fulfilled.

## How did Jesus Fulfill the Days of Awe?

The most basic way that Jesus fulfilled these days was to teach what true repentance is. He also taught what salvation is and how we "receive" it – instead of "achieving" it.

Jesus taught that repentance means turning in one's direction or changing one's mind. The words are *shub* or *nacham* in Hebrew and *metanoia* in the Greek. As the teachings of Jesus on repentance is developed in the New Testament, it is made clear that repentance involves a profound change in direction and in life, from sin and self-centeredness to holiness and God-centeredness.

The New Testament virtually begins with John the Baptist crying in the wilderness for men to repent of their evil ways (Matt. 3:2). Jesus began his public ministry by also preaching that men should repent (Matt. 4:17). In the New Testament, repentance is required before one can be baptized (Acts 2:38). It is the first step toward God after the Spirit's calling, and certainly involves a permanent change of mind and direction.

### Repentance Is: Turning Away From Sin

Repentance involves sorrow for our sins and for our sinful ways; however, it also involves a sorrow that will cause us to change these ways. Esau was sorrowful and he wept bitterly but his ways were not changed and he did not receive the promise (Heb. 12:16-17). The Bible tells us that there is a sorrow of this world that leads only to death, and a godly sorrow that leads to repentance and salvation (2 Cor. 7:10). It seems that much modern repentance is not of the godly sort. People today often repent only because they get caught in their sin, or they repent for other selfish reasons. As one old preacher said, "A lot of our repentance needs to be repented of." God desires that our hearts become broken over our sin. As the Jewish sage R. Nachman of Bratzlav said it, "There is none more whole than one with a broken heart (19)." Fortunately, the Holy Spirit is sent into the world to convict of sin (John 16:8). He will bring to light all these hidden things, and it is then our responsibility to turn from them.

### Repentance Is: Turning Toward God

Repentance is more than turning away from sin though. It is a positive and complete turning toward God and his kingdom. God is longing for all of us to repent in this fashion. In fact, the Bible says that *"now he commands all people everywhere to repent"* (Acts 17:30).

True repentance often involves restitution. That's something we can learn from Israel. The broken relationships with other people must be mended if repentance is sincere. Often we can't just say that we are sorry or just privately confess it to God and expect restoration. We need to show by our actions that there is a real and permanent change in our attitudes.

As Jesus passed through Jericho on his final journey to Jerusalem, he encountered a rich tax collector by the name of Zacchaeus. We can gather from the account that this rich man had a great desire to learn about Jesus and to follow him. When Jesus gave him the opportunity, he responded in this way, *"Look, Lord! Here and now I give half of my possessions to the poor, and if I have cheated anybody out of anything, I will pay back four times the amount"* (Luke 19:8). It is interesting that at this very point Jesus responded to him, *"Today salvation has come to this house..."* (v. 9). What Zacchaeus demonstrated was true biblical repentance, which often involves restitution for wrongs we have committed against others.

So in the Old Testament, a person who sinned against another couldn't just go to God and get forgiveness. He had to make up the loss that he had caused, and in addition he was required to add a fifth part to his restitution (Lev. 6:5; Num. 5:7). It would certainly change much of our repentance today if we had to make restitution plus 20% for all wrongs against others.

While repentance and reconciliation with God and man are important Scriptural teachings that all Christians are expected to practice, the degree to which we do these things and our success in them do not influence God concerning whether we are righteous or wicked. Jesus says in John 14:6 *"Jesus said to him, "I am the way, and the truth, and the life; no one comes to the Father but through Me."* Faith in Christ alone determines our state before God, nothing else.

Jesus always focused on God, and His "Awe-someness." Jesus essentially removed all need for the Days of Awe by showing us how we could never do anything to escape God's righteous judgment or gain God's favor and forgiveness. However, He also showed us how God lovingly gave us his love and forgiveness of sins and salvation through the sacrifice of His only Son, the Lord Jesus Christ!

### *Conclusion*

Today talk of repentance and sin is not politically correct. Often when we share the gospel, people often respond: 'But I'm a good person'. However, this belief does not match with Scripture which states: *'There is none who does good, no, not one'* (Psalm 14:3).

The Apostle Paul was constantly aware of his sin. He told Timothy, *'This is a faithful saying and worthy of all acceptance, that Christ Jesus came into the world to save sinners, of whom I am chief'* (1 Timothy 1:15). Paul was not keeping score of everyone's sins and calculating his as more numerous than everyone else's. He had a heart of continual repentance before the Lord. The closer we draw to God and His holiness, the more aware we are of our sin.

For the Christian, the Ten Days of Awe should be ten days of trying to see God's Awe, so fully that we should call this time 'Ten days of Ahhhhhhh." When we focus on the evil in our hearts and lives we feel discouraged! Why? Because we cannot change our status before a Holy God. What can wash away my sins? Nothing I can do! I can't apologize enough to all those whom I have hurt. Absolutely Nothing. I can't repent enough to deserve forgiveness from sin. Nothing, but the blood of Jesus. In Him, all things are new. He is Awesome. He is Forgiving. He is Merciful. He is loving. He is good. He is working *"all things together for good, for those who love Him and are called according to His purpose"*. Try as I may, I cannot search my spirit to know how I can be right with God, but by the power of His Spirit, He will bring to light the things that are hidden, and bring me to His forgiveness and to salvation. The period of the Days of Awe ends on the eve of the 10th day - Yom Kippur. This is the holiest day of the Jewish year.

*Who, O God, is like You? You forgive sins and overlook transgressions. For the survivors of Your people; He does not retain His anger forever, for He loves kindness; He will return and show us mercy, and overcome our sins, And You will cast into the depths of the sea all their sins; You will show kindness to Jacob and mercy to Abraham, As You did promise to our fathers of old. Micah (7:18-20)*

## *Footnotes for Chapter Seven*

1- As quoted in Rabbi Joseph Telushkin, *Jewish Literacy* , 623.

2- Judaism 101. http://www.jewfaq.org/elul.htm.

3- Nosson Scherman, Hersh Goldwurm and Avie Gold. *Rosh Hashanah – Its Significance, Laws and Prayers.* p. 15.

4- Louis Goldberg. *Our Jewish Friends.* p. 53.

5- Irving Greenberg. *The Jewish Way* . p. 186.

6- Ibid. p. 187.

7- Randy Weiss. *Cross Talk: Days of Awe – The Jewish High Holidays.* www.crosstalk.org/articles/awe.shtml.

8- Joseph Good. *Rosh Hashanah and the Messianic Kingdom to Come* . p. 90.

9- Ibid.

10- S.Y. Agnon. *Days of Awe* . p.109.

11- Elimelech David Ha-Levi. *Rosh Hashanah Traditional Greeting.* www.angelfire.com/pa2/passover/rosh-hashanah/traditional-greeting.

12-Joseph Good. *Rosh Hashanah and the Messianic Kingdom to Come* . p. 88.

15- Emden. *Siddur "Bet Ya'akob," ii* . 54b, 55a. (Prayers and Hymns used at Rosh Hashanah and the Days of Awe).

16- Bowker, John, *The Oxford Dictionary of World Religions* . p. 534.

17- Rabbi Jonathan Kraus . *Parashat "Ha'azinu"* (Sermon).

18- Randy Wise. *UnderstandingThe High Jewish Holy Days Of Rosh Hashanah And Yom Kippur.* www.mariechapian.com/teaching/ .

19- Jim Gerrish. *The Days Of Awe, A Study In Repentance* . Bridges For Peace Magazine, Jerusalem. 1993.

## Chapter Eight - Justification
### *Yom Kippur – Day of Atonement* (Tishri 10)

### First Blessing

*Blessed are You Adonai, Eternal One, Who enables us to welcome Yom Kippur by kindling these lights*

Three separate passages outline the Biblical observance of the Day of Atonement. First, God's instructions were given for the High Priest:

*Now the LORD spoke to Moses after the death of the two sons of Aaron, when they had approached the presence of the LORD and died. The LORD said to Moses: "Tell your brother Aaron that he shall not enter at any time into the holy place inside the veil, before the mercy seat which is on the ark, or he will die; for I will appear in the cloud over the mercy seat. Aaron shall enter the holy place with this: with a bull for a sin offering and a ram for a burnt offering. He shall put on the holy linen tunic, and the linen undergarments shall be next to his body, and he shall be girded with the linen sash and attired with the linen turban (these are holy garments) Then he shall bathe his body in water and put them on.*

*He shall take from the congregation of the sons of Israel two male goats for a sin offering and one ram for a burnt offering. Then Aaron shall offer the bull for the sin offering, which is for himself, that he may make atonement for himself and for his household. He shall take the two goats and present them before the LORD at the doorway of the tent of meeting. Aaron shall cast lots for the two goats, one lot for the LORD and the other lot for the scapegoat. Then Aaron shall offer the goat on which the lot for the LORD fell, and make it a sin offering. But the goat on which the lot for the scapegoat fell shall be presented alive before the LORD, to make atonement upon it, to send it into the wilderness as the scapegoat. Then Aaron shall offer the bull of the sin offering which is for himself and make atonement for himself and for his household, and he shall slaughter the bull of the sin offering which is for himself. ---- Leviticus 16:1-34 (due to its length the entire text is not included here.)*

Second, there are instructions given for the people:

*The LORD said to Moses, "The tenth day of this seventh month is the Day of Atonement. Hold a sacred assembly and deny yourselves, and present an offering made to the LORD by fire. Do no work on that day, because it is the Day of Atonement, when atonement is made for you before the LORD your God. Anyone who does not deny himself on that day must be cut off from his people. I will destroy from among his people anyone who does any work on that day. You shall do no work at all. This is to be a lasting ordinance for the generations to come, wherever you live. It is a Sabbath of rest for you, and you must deny yourselves. From the evening of the ninth day of the month until the following evening you are to observe your Sabbath." - Leviticus 23:26-32*

Thirdly, there are the instructions given for the sacrifices:

*Then on the tenth day of this seventh month you shall have a holy convocation, and you shall humble yourselves; you shall not do any work. You shall present a burnt offering to the LORD as a soothing aroma: one bull, one ram, seven male lambs one year old, having them without defect; and their grain offering, fine flour mixed with oil: three-tenths of an ephah for the bull, two-tenths for the one ram, a tenth for each of the seven lambs; one male goat for a sin offering, besides the sin offering of atonement and the continual burnt offering and its grain offering, and their drink offerings. – Numbers 29:7-11*

The New Testament refers to this day in Hebrews:

*...but into the second (room), only the high priest enters once a year, not without taking blood, which he offers for himself and for the sins of the people committed in ignorance....But when Christ appeared as a high priest of the good things to come,...He entered not through the blood of goats and calves, but through His own blood, He entered the holy place once for all, having obtained eternal redemption. Hebrews 9:7, 11-12*

The Day of Atonement is the English equivalent of Yom Kippur. "Atonement" is Kippur in Hebrew and Kippur is from the Hebrew word kaphar, which means "to ransom" or "to cover". So in defining the word, atonement means a covering. It was on Yom Kippur that atonement (covering) was made for the previous year's sins. The atonement or covering consisted of a blood sacrifice of an innocent animal. The Lord Commanded, *"For the life of the flesh is in the blood, and I have given it to you on the altar to make atonement for your souls; for it is the blood by reason of the life that makes atonement.' (Leviticus 17:11)*

### *When is the Day of Atonement?*

The Day of Atonement is connected to the High Holy Days. The Feast of Trumpets begins these days on Tishri 1. Then there are the ten Days of Awe. Then the Day of Atonement occurs on Tishri 10. After this holiday comes the Feast of Tabernacles on Tishri 15. Tishri is the equivalent of September or October and so this feast always occurs in the autumn of the year. Yom Kippur or Day of Atonement is the Sabbath of Sabbaths.

The first Yom Kippur took place after Moses returned from his second trip to Mt. Sinai with the replacement set of tablets containing the Ten Commandments. He had broken the original set when he returned the first time to discover the children of Israel worshipping a golden calf rather than God, who brought them out from Egypt. The Jews refer to this day as the Day of Forgiveness. Not only is this the day God forgives our sins but also the historical day on which God forgave the people and gave them a second set of the ten commandments on stone **(1).**

Moses successfully pleaded with God on their behalf, and on the first of Elul, he ascended the mountain, this time for a second set of tablets. In Moses' absence, the nation fasted from sunrise to sunset. Moses descended the mountain on the tenth of Tishri. Upon returning, Moses found the nation truly repentant and announced that God had forgiven them. God decreed that the tenth of Tishri would remain a day of atonement for all generations.

*And this shall be an eternal law for you. Each year on the tenth day of the seventh month you must fast and do no work. This is true of the native born and of the proselyte who comes to join you. This is because on this day you shall have all your sins atoned, so that you will be cleansed. Before God you will be cleansed of your sins. It is a Sabbath of Sabbaths to you, and a day upon which you must fast. This is a law for all time. (Leviticus 16:29-31)*

Later, following the completion of the portable wilderness tabernacle the Israelites were commanded to build in the desert, Moses, through direct communication with God, instructed the people in the tabernacle's service and rituals. In time, this became the basis for the priestly duties performed during the first and second temple era. Following the sin of the golden calf, the Israelites who wandered the desert, understood that the private and communal actions taken every Yom Kippur helped ensure annual atonement for their sins (2).

### *What Is the Day of Atonement?*

This is Israel's most awesome holy day. It has been observed for 3500 years and to this day wields a powerful influence of the culture and worship of Israel. More importantly, the Day of Atonement provides a necessary backdrop for understanding the scope of the Messiah's payment for sin and the security of God's people today (3).

The Day of Atonement," is a day set aside to "afflict the soul," to atone for the sins of the past year. In the Days of Awe, I mentioned the "books" in which God inscribes all of our names. On Yom Kippur, the judgment entered in these books is sealed. This day is, essentially, your last appeal, your last chance to change the judgment, to demonstrate your repentance and make amends.

As I noted in Days of Awe, Yom Kippur atones for sins only between man and God, not for sins against another person. To atone for sins against another person, you must first seek reconciliation with that person, righting the wrongs you committed against them if possible. That must all be done before Yom Kippur (4).

### What is the Meaning of the Day of Atonement?

The purpose of killing an innocent animal was not to solely blame it for the collective sins of the people. It was a kind of vehicle through which one could transport those sins and transgressions far away. Divine forgiveness was only possible after the entire congregation acknowledged and sought forgiveness for their behavior. It was also a symbolic reminder of what God could do to them if they did not repent. And it was a reminder that there is no forgiveness of sins apart from the shedding of blood. *"And according to the Law, one may almost say, all things are cleansed with blood, and without shedding of blood there is no forgiveness." (Hebrews 9:22)*

This kind of transference ritual provided the basis for the Jewish custom of atonements. The belief that somehow sins can be transferred from human to animal has been a controversial subject among rabbis. As a result, this ceremony is no longer (except among the very ultra-orthodox or Hasidic circles) practiced today. Instead, repentance, prayer and giving charity are the accepted Jewish practices for obtaining divine forgiveness. This is also one reason why the Rabbis cannot accept Jesus as Messiah. He had to die to bring salvation – all our sins were transferred to Him. This is an unacceptable concept to them. And yet the Torah says in Yoma 5a "There is no atonement except with blood" (5). The New Testament also says this in Hebrews 9:22 "Without the shedding of blood there is no forgiveness."

As far as scholars can tell, the only time Yom Kippur rituals were suspended was during the dedication of the second temple by King Solomon, which began two days before the holiday and continued through Sukkot, The Feast of Tabernacles, with food, drink and festivities.

### How was the Day of Atonement to be celebrated?

#### In the Desert:
In the desert, Moses' older brother, Aaron, assumed the role of High Priest. Through washing, vestment changes and the sacrificial blood of animals chosen "for God," the High Priest was able to purify himself, his family and his

nation. In addition, the High Priest purified the Holy of Holies, the curtained-off area of the tabernacle, which contained the tablets of the moral law, over which the Shechinah , or glory of the Spirit of God, hovered like a cloud.

Using a goat, called *Azazel*, often translated as scapegoat, the High Priest would place his hands on its head and confess the sins of the nation, essentially laying the blame on the head of the animal. The goat was then pushed off a high cliff to fall to its death (6).

Yom Kippur is a complete Sabbath; no work can be performed on that day. Once the holiday candles are lit, Yom Kippur and its five prohibitions take effect. From sunset to sunset, there is no eating and drinking (even water). It is a complete, 25-hour fast beginning before sunset on the evening before Yom Kippur and ending after nightfall on the day of Yom Kippur. This is the only fast that is mandated in the Torah (7).

The Talmud also specifies additional restrictions that are less well-known: washing and bathing, anointing one's body (with cosmetics, deodorants, etc.), wearing leather shoes (Orthodox Jews today routinely wear canvas sneakers under their dress clothes on Yom Kippur), and engaging in sexual relations are all prohibited on Yom Kippur. However, children not yet bar or bat-mitzvah, women who are pregnant or nursing, and anyone who is sick or infirm, may eat and drink as needed **(8).**

Having said all this however, it is important to note that Yom Kippur, the Day of Atonement was meant to be a joyous day. It is frequently perceived as a day of sadness because of the seriousness of the day and because it was the harshest fast day of the year and because of the other restrictions on this day. However, the Rabbis wrote in the Talmud, "There were no happier days for the Jewish people as the fifteenth of Av (a day on which marriages were arranged) and Yom Kippur (9)."

Most of the holiday is spent in the synagogue, in prayer. In Orthodox synagogues, services begin early in the morning (8 or 9 AM) and continue until about 3 PM. People then usually go home for an afternoon nap and return around 5 or 6 PM for the afternoon and evening services, which continue until nightfall. The services end at nightfall, with the blowing of a long blast on the shofar. It is customary to wear white on the holiday, which symbolizes purity and calls to mind the promise that our sins shall be made as white as snow (Is. 1:18). Some people wear a *kittel* , the white robe in which the dead are buried (10).

### In The First and Second Temple Era:

Much is written about Yom Kippur's observance during the Second Temple era. Seven of the eight chapters of the Talmud tractate Yoma detail the High Priest's temple service. The books Ecclesiastics and Jubilees, which were written in the second century B.C.; texts found in the Qumran Caves near the Dead Sea; and, the works of Philo of Alexandria, the Hellenistic philosopher who lived in Egypt during the later years of the second temple, corroborate the writings of Talmudic sages. For the most part, however, the Day of Atonement was celebrated in the same way as it had been in the Wilderness Tabernacle.

Yom Kippur was so important that those who were not able to worship in Jerusalem spent the entire day in their local synagogues refraining from food and drink. Even those not religious, made an exception for Yom Kippur. For the many who did make the trek to Jerusalem, an awesome experience was waiting.

### In Jesus Day:

Since the first of Elul, more than a month before Yom Kippur, all of the customs, traditions, introspection, prayers, even foods, have been a kind of dress rehearsal for Yom Kippur: the day Jewish fate is sealed.

### Confession:

The confessional is said during the afternoon prayers on the day before Yom Kippur. It is a custom for men to wear white. Although the confession is repeated throughout Yom Kippur, it was thought that if one should die later that day, perhaps over something eaten before the fast, one would have already recited the confessional and sought forgiveness **(11)**.

### The final meal:

Since Yom Kippur is the toughest fast day of the Jewish calendar, (about 25 hours) the rabbis thought to add a little festivity to the day before. The Talmud, in Tractate Yoma (81b), says, "Just as it is a mitzvah to fast on the tenth of Tishri, so is it a mitzvah to eat on the ninth (12)."

The meal, which is similar to a traditional Sabbath meal, with soup and chicken, takes place before sunset and before synagogue services. *Kiddush* , the prayer over wine, is not recited, but the blessing over the traditional Jewish bread, is: "Blessed are you king of the universe who delivers forth bread from the earth."

### The Temple Service:

A week before the holiday, the High Priest would leave his home to live inside the temple. That week, he would perform all the temple duties himself. In addition, he would study two Torah portions and learn one by heart to make sure he didn't make any mistakes. The night before, the High Priest would stay up all night learning Torah and preparing himself spiritually. If he fell asleep, young priests woke him up by reciting psalms. Sometimes they would make the High Priest stand all night on the cold, stone floor.

In the morning, he would put on his priestly clothes and go about the daily morning service, including the morning's sacrifice, the lighting of the menorah and the burning of incense. Then he would wash his hands and feet in a golden basin. Afterwards, he took a bath, a ritual he repeated throughout the day.

Then, the High Priest would change into a simple robe made of white linen and walk over to a young bull and recite for himself and for his family the first of three confessional prayers. Three times during the prayer he pronounced the *Shem Hameforash* , (the name by which God identified himself to Moses at the burning bush, and to this day, remains unpronounceable), instead of the usual "Adonai," meaning Lord.

The crowd of worshipers, in awe of the moment, fell on the floor, and cried out in loud voices, "Blessed be the Name, the glory of His kingdom forever and ever", a phrase, that even today, is only said out loud on Yom Kippur.

The High Priest then walked over to two identical goats. Through a lottery, one goat was chosen as a sacrifice to God, and the other, a scapegoat, with red wool tied around its horns, was sent out into the wilderness, a symbol of the collective sins of the people. The young goat was then slaughtered and its blood collected in a basin for later use.

Then came the most important part of the ceremony. The High Priest walked up a special ramp (so temple priests could ascend with modesty in tact) to the altar, filled a gold pan with coals and a golden ladle with incense. Then, with the blood of the bullock and with everyone watching, he walked into the Holy of Holies, the inner sanctuary where God's Spirit dwelled and where no one but the High Priest entered and he only entered on Yom Kippur. Once inside, he lit the incense, sprinkled the blood of the bullock on the Mercy Seat and in front of the Ark of the Covenant and if all went well, emerged unscathed from the inner chamber.

The ritual continued with the High Priest sprinkling blood on the curtain of the Holy of Holies as an act of purification. Next, the remaining goat was slaughtered, and some of its blood was taken by the High Priest into the Holy of Holies and sprinkled on the Mercy Seat and in front of the Ark of the Covenant for the sins of the people. Then additional blood sprinkled on the curtain and around the base of the altar.

The scapegoat was then led through the temple's gate to a waiting priest whose job it was to take it to predetermined spot about ten to twelve miles away. Along the way, there were ten stations with food or drink in case the tired priest needed to break his fast. When the priest came to the final station, he pushed the goat off a cliff. Using a system of signal flags, the priest leading the animal would message back to the temple that the sins of the people were forgiven (supposedly the red wool around the goat's horns turned miraculously white) **(13)**.

### Afternoon Service:

Although the special Yom Kippur service was concluded, the regular afternoon temple service still had to be completed. The High Priest again washed and changed his clothes, lit the menorah and burned the incense.

When he finally went home, well wishers, who after praying and fasting all day, wanted to thank the High Priest for a successful Yom Kippur, accompanied him. At home, however, he could still not relax. As High Priest, it was his duty to invite fellow priests and dignitaries to a feast. Today, when families return home from the long day of fasting and praying, they also come home to break-the-fast meal, usually dairy, joined by family and friends.

### An interesting anecdote:

It was also the custom following Yom Kippur, for unmarried young men and women to go dancing in the vineyards to find mates. All the young women wore white so the rich would not have an advantage over the poor who could not afford finer clothes. In the Talmud, Rabbi Simeon Ben Gamaliel is quoted as saying; "There were no happier days in Israel than the fifteenth of Av and Yom Kippur." This is probably the basis today for many Jewish communities which host single's dances right after Yom Kippur.

### Post Temple Era

After the destruction of the second temple in 70 A.D., the rabbis faced the difficult challenge of keeping the service and rituals of Yom Kippur intact for future generations. The rabbis had to reconstruct the day without the pageantry associated with temple life.

Emphasis had to shift from sacrifices and priestly rituals to prayer, repentance and giving of charity. But, because of the historic importance of the day, and the people's memory, the rabbis retained descriptions of the rituals in the Yom Kippur service, now referred to as the *Avodah*. The *mahtzor*, (the special prayer-book used on Yom Kippur), and the temple services it recounts, have taken the place of the actual sacrifices and rituals whose origins date back to the Israelites in the desert and to the Jews of the first and second temple era **(14)** .

### *How did Jesus fulfill the Day of Atonement?*

Christians know that Jesus has provided our atonement: *"...for all have sinned and come short of the glory of God; being justified freely by his grace through the redemption that is in Christ Jesus" (Rom. 2:23-24)* . God presented Him as a sacrifice of atonement, through faith in His blood. Jesus' death surpasses and replaces the atonement ritual of the Jewish Temple. The book of Hebrews explains the ceremonies of the Day of Atonement as a pattern of the atoning work of Christ. Jesus is our high priest, and His blood shed on Calvary is seen as symbolized in the blood of bulls and goats. As the high priest of the Old Testament entered the Holy of Holies with the blood of his sacrificial victim, so Jesus entered heaven itself to appear before the Father on behalf of His people (Heb. 9:11-12).

The Old Testament tabernacle was designed, in part, to teach Israel that sin hindered access to the presence of God. Only the high priest, and he only once a year, could enter the Holy of Holies, and then not without taking blood offered to atone for sins (Heb. 9:7). Hebrews notes that the Levitical offerings could effect only the purification of the flesh. They ceremonially cleansed the sinner, but they could not bring about inward cleansing, the prerequisite for fellowship with God. Just as the high priest had to be symbolically sinless through the sacrifice of the bullock to enter the Holy of Holies and live, so Jesus had to be sinless to live after He entered the grave. *But when Christ appeared as a high priest of the good things to come, He entered through the greater and more perfect tabernacle, not made with hands, that is to say, not of this creation; and not through the blood of goats and calves, but through His own blood, He entered the holy place once for all, having obtained eternal redemption. For if the blood of goats and bulls and the ashes of a heifer sprinkling those who have been defiled sanctify for the cleansing of the flesh, how much more will the blood of Christ, who through the eternal Spirit offered Himself without blemish to God, cleanse your conscience from dead works to serve the living God (Heb. 9:11-14)?*

The high priest had to offer sin offerings each year for his own sins and the sins of the people. This annual repetition of the sacrifices served as a reminder that perfect atonement had not yet been provided. Jesus, however, through His own blood, effected eternal redemption for His people (Heb. 9:12).

The Old Testament offerings served as a pattern and a prophecy of Jesus, who, through His better sacrifice, cleanses the conscience from dead works (Heb. 9:13-14). God always determined what was an acceptable offering and what was not. He finally provided His Son, the Lamb of God, as the sacrifice for the sins of the world (John 1:19; 3:16). The moment Jesus died, the veil of the temple was torn in two, from top to bottom (Matt. 27:50-51). The earth quaked beneath men's feet. This event is important because it established Jesus as being the new High Priest and Lamb of God. No longer must there be an annual sacrifice for sin on our behalf; instead, He has made payment for us once and for all. Jesus, through a new and living way has entered heaven itself, the true Holy of Holies, where He ever lives to make intercession for His people. The believer need not stand afar off, as did the Israelite of old, but may now, through Christ, approach the very Throne of Grace! Yes, it is now possible for each of us to have direct access to God through the blood of Jesus Christ! Praise the Lord!!

### The Two Goats

After purifying the holy place and the altar of burnt offering with the mingled blood of the bullock, the High Priest went to the eastern side of the court in front of the Temple. Facing him were two identical goats. Nearby was a lottery box especially designed for this ceremony. In the box were two tablets (lots). One bore the name "For God," the other "For azazel" (the scapegoat). The high priest shook the box and withdrew the tablets, putting one tablet in front of each goat. The goat labeled "for God" was sacrificed. The priest laid his hands upon the goat's head labeled "for azazel" and confessed over it the sins of Israel. The scapegoat symbolically bore the sins of the nation of Israel away from the people. This goat, commonly called the scapegoat (i.e. escape goat), was then driven into the desert (15).

In the same way Jesus was brought before Pilate and stood before the people just as He was about to be led forth, bearing the iniquities of the people. These two goats were required for one sacrifice (Lev 16:17, 21-22). Both sacrifices were fulfilled in the death and resurrection of Jesus. How can resurrection be portrayed in a sacrifice? By using two animals, one killed, the other set free, representing Jesus' death and resurrection.

*And he shall take the two goats, and present them before the LORD at the door of the tabernacle of the congregation. And Aaron shall cast lots upon the two goats; one lot for the LORD, and the other lot for the scapegoat. And Aaron shall bring the goat upon which the LORD'S lot fell, and offer him for a sin offering. But the goat, on which the lot fell to be the scapegoat, shall be presented alive before the LORD, to make an atonement with him, and to let him go for a scapegoat into the wilderness (Lev. 16:7-10).*

*And he shall go out unto the altar that is before the LORD, and make an atonement for it; and shall take of the blood of the bullock, and of the blood of the goat, and put it upon the horns of the altar round about. And the goat shall bear upon him all their iniquities unto a land not inhabited: and he shall let go the goat in the wilderness (Lev. 16:18, 22).*

Tradition states that a cord of red wool was tied on the horn of the scapegoat, before it was let go in the wilderness. When the red wool turned white, it was a sign that God forgave the people's sin. *Come now, and let us reason together, saith the LORD: though your sins be as scarlet, they shall be as white as snow; though they be red like crimson, they shall be as wool (Isa. 1:18).*

The Priests used to bind a shining crimson strip of cloth on the outside door of the Temple. If the strip of cloth turned into the white color, they would rejoice; if it did not turn white they were full of sorrow and shame. Amazingly, Jewish literature goes on to declare that the Shechinah glory of God left the Temple forty years prior to its destruction. Three signs occurred to show evidence of this: 1) The western candle of the menorah refused to burn continually. 2) The doors of the Temple would open of themselves. 3) The red wool no longer turned white supernaturally. This is especially significant because it indicated that God was no longer forgiving the sins of His people. The people were sorrowful because they began to realize more and more that the sacrifice of Yom Kippur did not have the power to cleanse their sinful hearts. When Jesus started His ministry and completed His salvation work, the blood of bulls and goats was no longer accepted as a sacrifice for the atonement of sin (16)!

### Conclusion

"Atonement" means a covering. It was on Yom Kippur that atonement (covering) was made for the previous year's sins. The atonement or covering consisted of a blood sacrifice of an innocent animal. The Lord Commanded, *"For the life of the flesh is in the blood, and I have given it to you on the altar to make atonement for your souls; for it is the blood by reason of the life that makes atonement.' (Leviticus 17:11).*

When Jesus came He did not just cover our sins, He removed them and He removed them permanently. His was the sacrifice promised in Genesis 3:15 and it was perfect and complete. When He died on the cross His last words were "It is finished". He did not mean "now I am dead," He meant, "all that is necessary for the restoration of God's people to Himself has now been completed and accomplished." No other sacrifice would ever be needed before the Heavenly Father nor would any other sacrifice ever again be accepted. Salvation had been accomplished! Praise the Lord! *But when Christ appeared as a high priest of the good things to come, He entered through the greater and more perfect tabernacle, not made with hands, that is to say, not of this creation; and not through the blood of goats and calves, but through His own blood, He entered the holy place once for all, having obtained eternal redemption. For if the blood of goats and bulls and the ashes of a heifer sprinkling those who have been defiled sanctify for the cleansing of the flesh, how much more will the blood of Christ, who through the eternal Spirit offered Himself without blemish to God, cleanse your conscience from dead works to serve the living God (Heb. 9:11-14)?*

### Second Blessing
Blessed are You O Lord Our God, King of the universe,
Who has kept us alive, sustained us, and encouraged us
To observe this day.

# Footnotes for Chapter Eight:

1- chabad.org/calendar/view/day.htm/aid/142130/jewish/Jewish-Calendar.html

2-Everything Jewish. http://www.everythingjewish.com/YomK/YK_origins.htm
3- Kevin Howard and Marvin Rosenthal. The Feasts of the Lord . p. 120.
4- Judaism 101, http://www.jewfaq.org/holiday4.htm
5- Victor Buksbazen. The Gospel in the Feasts of Israel . p. 31.
6-Everything Jewish. http://www.everythingjewish.com/YomK/YK_origins.htm
7- Joseph Tulushkin. Jewish Literacy. p. 569.
8- Ibid.
9- Mishnah, Yoma 8:9.
10- Judaism 101, http://www.jewfaq.org/holiday4.htm
11- Daniel Kohn. Prayer Services for Yom Kippur. My Jewish Learning Inc.,
    2006.
12- Michael Strassfeld. The Jewish Holidays, A Guide & Commentary . p.112.
13- Daniel Kohn. Prayer Services for Yom Kippur. My Jewish Learning Inc.,
    2006.
14- Amy J. Kramer. Yom Kippur: Origins. trialsofgrizelda.com/harvest/yom
    %20kippur15- Biblical Holidays, http://biblicalholidays.com/
    messiah_in_yom_kippur.htm
16- Torah Tractate Yoma 67a

*Feast of Tabernacles*

*33 The LORD said to Moses, 34 "Say to the Israelites: 'On the fifteenth day of the seventh month the LORD's Feast of Tabernacles begins, and it lasts for seven days. 35 The first day is a sacred assembly; do no regular work. 36 For seven days present offerings made to the LORD by fire, and on the eighth day hold a sacred assembly and present an offering made to the LORD by fire. It is the closing assembly; do no regular work. 37 ("'These are the LORD's appointed feasts, which you are to proclaim as sacred assemblies for bringing offerings made to the LORD by fire—the burnt offerings and grain offerings, sacrifices and drink offerings required for each day. 38 These offerings are in addition to those for the LORD's Sabbaths and in addition to your gifts and whatever you have vowed and all the freewill offerings you give to the LORD.) 39 " 'So beginning with the fifteenth day of the seventh month, after you have gathered the crops of the land, celebrate the festival to the LORD for seven days; the first day is a day of rest, and the eighth day also is a day of rest. 40 On the first day you are to take choice fruit from the trees, and palm fronds, leafy branches and poplars, and rejoice before the LORD your God for seven days. 41 Celebrate this as a festival to the LORD for seven days each year. This is to be a lasting ordinance for the generations to come; celebrate it in the seventh month. 42 Live in booths for seven days: All native-born Israelites are to live in booths 43 so your descendants will know that I had the Israelites live in booths when I brought them out of Egypt. I am the LORD your God.' " 44 So Moses announced to the Israelites the appointed feasts of the LORD. (Lev. 23:33-44)*

The number of days between Nisan and Tishri is always the same. Because of this, the time from the first major festival (Passover in Nisan) to the last major festival (The Feast of Tabernacles in Tishri) is always the same. Passover is in the first month in the religious calendar and Tabernacles is in the first month of the civil calendar. Hosea 6:3 explains *Then shall we know, if we follow on to know the LORD: his going forth is prepared as the morning; and he shall come unto us as the rain, as the latter and former rain unto the earth.* The spring holidays are during the former rain and the fall holidays are during the latter rain.

This same concept of rain is used as a punishment as well. Those who forsake attending the Feast of Tabernacles will receive no rain " *16 And it shall come to pass, that every one that is left of all the nations which came against Jerusalem shall even go up from year to year to worship the King, the LORD of hosts, and to keep the feast of tabernacles. 17 And it shall be, that whoso will not come up of all the families of the earth unto Jerusalem to worship the King,* the LORD of hosts, even upon them shall be no rain." *(Zechariah 14:16-17)* *(1)*. So the Feast of Tabernacles was a very important end to the annual festival season of the nation of Israel and the people of God.

For the Israelites living in Biblical times, the holidays were concentrated in two months: the first month of the year, Nisan, incorporated Passover, Unleavened Bread and First Fruits; and the seventh month Tishri incorporated the Feast of Trumpets, the Day of Atonement and the Feast of Tabernacles. Nisan celebrates the beginning of salvation of the people and Tishri celebrates the beginning of the Nation of Israel. So Nisan is the Spiritual New Year and Tishri is the Civil New Year. However, both months were dominated by the Exodus holidays – Passover and Tabernacles.

The only other holiday was Pentecost, which occurred in the third month. Passover, marking the liberation, and Tabernacles, commemorating the journey, are the highlight events in the Hebrew Calendar. Pentecost is the link between the two major Exodus commemorations, marking the transformation of Exodus from a one time event into an ongoing commitment (2).

The Feast of Tabernacles celebrates the redemption way itself, for the Jews. Tabernacles reconstruct the wilderness trek, the long journey to the Promised Land. If as the prophet said, in the absence of a vision the people perishes, then the trek can truly affirm that in the constant presence of our vision, a people lives on eternally (3).

### When is the Feast of Tabernacles?

The Feast of Tabernacles is a weeklong autumn harvest festival. The Feast of Tabernacles is also known as the Feast of the Ingathering, Feast of the Booths, Sukkoth, Succoth, or Sukkot (variations in spellings occur because these words are transliterations of the Hebrew word pronounced "Sue-coat"). The two days following the festival are separate holidays, Shemini Atzeret and Simkhat Torah, but are commonly thought of as part of the Feast of Tabernacles.

The Feast of Tabernacles was the final and most important holiday of the year. The importance of this festival is indicated by the statement, *"This is to be a lasting ordinance."* The divine pronouncement , *"I am the Lord your God,"* concludes this section on the holidays of the seventh month. The Feast of Tabernacles begins five days after Yom Kippur on the fifteenth of Tishri (September or October). It is a drastic change from one of the most solemn holidays in the year to one of the most joyous. The word Sukkoth means "booths," and refers to the temporary dwellings that Jews are commanded to live in during this holiday, just as the Jews did in the wilderness. The Feast of

Tabernacles lasts for seven days and ends on the twenty-first day of the Hebrew month of Tishri, which is Israel's seventh month **(4)**.

This holiday has a dual significance: historical and agricultural (just as Passover and Pentecost). Historically, it was to be kept in remembrance of the dwelling in tents in the wilderness for the forty-year period during which the children of Israel were wandering in the desert. It is expounded in Leviticus 23:43 That *"your generations may know that I made the children of Israel to dwell in booths, when I brought them out of the land of Egypt: I am the LORD your God (5)."* Agriculturally, Tabernacles is a harvest festival and is sometimes referred to as the Festival of Ingathering.

### *What were they to remember?*

Matthew Henry's commentary explains; The people were to remember; 1) The poverty of their beginning, and the low and desolate state out of which God advanced that people, and 2) The mercy of God to them, that, when they dwelt in tabernacles, God not only set up a tabernacle for Himself among them, but, with the utmost care and tenderness imaginable, hung a canopy over them, even the cloud that sheltered them from the heat of the sun. God's former mercies to us and our fathers ought to be kept in everlasting remembrance.

The eighth day was the great day of this holiday, because then they returned to their own houses again, and remembered how, after they had long dwelt in tents in the wilderness, at length they came to a happy settlement in the land of promise, where they dwelt in goodly houses. And they would more sensibly value and be thankful for the comforts and conveniences of their houses when they had spent seven days dwelling in booths. It is good for those that have ease and plenty sometimes to learn what it is to endure hardness.

The people were to keep this holiday in thankfulness to God for all the increase of the year; however, the emphasis is that Israel's life rested upon redemption, which in its ultimate meaning is the forgiveness of sin. This fact separates this holiday from the harvest festivals of the neighboring nations whose roots lay in the mythological activity of the gods.

### *What Is the Feast of Tabernacles?*

It is one of the three pilgrim feasts of Israel when all the males in Israel must go to the temple. It is so unreservedly joyful that it is commonly referred to in Jewish prayer and literature as the Season of our Rejoicing. Tabernacles was also a joyful commemoration of the divine guidance granted to the Atonement, the idea of joy after redemption was naturally very prominent.

It also became a designated time for giving special thanks for the harvest of the fields and newborn livestock of the year. It could be rightly viewed as the biblical "Thanksgiving" holiday. This feast was the completion of the sacred cycle of Israel's year as well as the agricultural or working year. It also marked the change of seasons, the approach of rain and the winter equinox, and determined alike the commencement and the close of a sabbatical year (Deut. 31:10).

The Feast of Tabernacles came 5 days after the Day of Atonement. It occurred on the 15th day of the month that is at the full moon, when the sacred month had attained its full strength. On the Day of Atonement the sin of Israel had been removed and its covenant relationship to God had been restored. Thus a holy nation could keep a holy feast of harvest joy unto the Lord, just as in the truest sense it will be "in that future day" (Zechariah 4:20) when the meaning of the Feasts of Tabernacles shall be really and finally fulfilled (6).

### *How was the Feast of Tabernacles to be Celebrated?*

As The Feast of Tabernacles approached, the entire Jewish nation started making preparations. Work crews were sent to repair roads and bridges for the thousands of pilgrims coming to Jerusalem. During the festival many Jews eat (and sleep, as well) in booths or huts, which are built in the five days between Yom Kippur and this festival.

The Feast of Tabernacles is by far the most festive and joyous of occasions. History records that four huge candelabra were constructed, lighted, and attended by young men ascending ladders periodically with pitchers of oil to keep them burning. The light from these lamps illuminated the whole city, and around them danced distinguished men with torches in their hands, singing hymns and songs of praise. The dancing as well as the music continued until daybreak. It was an extravaganza! The Rabbis called it simply "the holiday"(7).

The holiday was celebrated following the outline in Leviticus: They lived in booths made of boughs of trees and branches of palm trees for the seven days of the feast (Lev. 23:42) and each person carried in his hands a *lulav*, consisting of palm-branches, or willows of the brook, and fruits of peach and citron.. They rested from all regular work on the first and eighth days. The Priest offered sacrifices on the seven days, beginning with thirteen bullocks and other animals on the first day and diminishing by one bullock each day until, on the seventh, seven bullocks were offered. On the eighth day there was a solemn assembly when one bullock, one ram, and seven lambs were offered (Num. 29:36). The sacrifices offered during this time amounted to 189 animals. Men carried the cluster of branches to the synagogue to wave as they rejoiced before the Lord, as commanded by the Lord (Lev. 23:40).

Water was also an important part of the Feast of Tabernacles. Before the festival, the Rabbis taught on every passage in Scripture dealing with water. In Old Testament Biblical times, gold pitchers of water were brought from the pool of Siloam to the temple. The Priest would pour out the water over the altar to signify Israel's gratitude for the rain that had produced the harvest, and would pray for rain in the next year. The priest would recite Isaiah 12:1-3. *And in that day thou shalt say, O LORD, I will praise thee: though thou wast angry with me, thine anger is turned away, and thou comfortedst me . Behold, God is my salvation; I will trust, and not be afraid: for the LORD JEHOVAH is my strength and my song; he also is become my salvation. Therefore with joy shall ye draw water out of the wells of salvation.*

This special libation was performed only during the seven days of the Feast of Tabernacles. This was done not only to remind God of the need for abundant rain during the winter season, but also to remind the people of the coming Messiah who had promised to pour out His Holy Spirit on the people.

The last day of the Feast was called Hosha'na Rabba, meaning the Day of the Great Hosanna. As the celebration continued, the priests blew the trumpets and waved the branches and the people sang the Great Hallel (Psalms 113 through 118). This was also the time when the people brought their tithes and offerings to the Temple because they were not to "appear before the Lord empty-handed (Deut. 16:16).

In addition the people of Israel celebrated the dedication of the Temple built by King Solomon. At that observance of the holiday (2 Chron. 5:3) the Shekinah glory of the Lord descended from heaven to light the fire on the altar and fill the Holy of Holies (I Kings 8: 3; 2 Chron. 7:1-10).

The two most important ceremonies of the feast – the pouring of water and the illumination of the temple with the enormous lamps - were representative of the pillar of cloud by day and the tower of fire by night over the Wilderness Tabernacle according to Jewish tradition. This tradition also states that the cloud and fire began appearing over the Wilderness Tabernacle on the 15th of Tishri, the first day of this feast. Previously on that day Moses was said to have down from Mt. Sinai and announced to the people that the Tabernacle of God was to be reared among them.

This feast is also alluded to in Rev. 7:9, 10 speaking of the future day of the Lord " *After this I beheld, and, lo, a great multitude, which no man could number, of all nations, and kindreds, and people, and tongues, stood before the throne, and before the Lamb, clothed with white robes, and palms in their hands; And cried with a loud voice, saying, Salvation to our God which sitteth upon the throne, and unto the Lamb (8)."*

### How did Jesus fulfill the Feast of Tabernacles?

There was some debate over Jesus going to this feast. John 7:10-26 says: " *1 After this, Jesus went around in Galilee, purposely staying away from Judea because the Jews there were waiting to take his life. 2 But when the Jewish Feast of Tabernacles was near, 3 Jesus' brothers said to him, "You ought to leave here and go to Judea, so that your disciples may see the miracles you do. 4 No one who wants to become a public figure acts in secret. Since you are doing these things, show yourself to the world." 5 For even his own brothers did not believe in him. 6 Therefore Jesus told them, "The right time for me has not yet come; for you any time is right. 7 The world cannot hate you, but it hates me because I testify that what it does is evil. 8 You go to the Feast. I am not yet going up to this Feast, because for me the right time has not yet come." 9 Having said this, he stayed in Galilee. 10 However, after his brothers had left for the Feast, he went also, not publicly, but in secret*

It was now the third year of Jesus' special work for God, and it was autumn. Six months after this, Jesus would die on the cross. Every time that Jesus went to Jerusalem there was more danger for him. The men who ruled the Jews in Jerusalem were enemies of Jesus and they now wanted to kill him as soon as possible.

On a previous visit to Jerusalem, Jesus had cured a man at the Pool of Bethesda. The man had not been able to walk for 38 years and not only did Jesus heal him but He cured the man on the Sabbath. This made the Pharisees in particular very angry. They thought that nobody should do any work on the Sabbath under any circumstances (John 5). And then, when Jesus discussed this with them, He called God his own father and so linked himself with God. This made Him equal with God (John 5:16-18) and so the Priests, the enemies of Jesus plotted to kill him.

Probably there were other reasons why they hated Jesus. Jesus had taught people how God wanted them to live. He taught them that God's standards were different from men's standards. He showed the people that their leaders' and rulers' standards were not good enough. Other people could see this, and the rulers were losing their power so Jesus was in danger at Jerusalem. However, to obey the Jewish law (Deut. 16:16) that all males should go to Jerusalem meant Jesus also had to go. So, people asked, 'would Jesus go or not?' If Jesus went, nobody expected his safe return. But Jesus did go to the Feast and in so doing He fulfilled all the various aspects of it.

## What Did Jesus Do To Fulfill The Feast of Tabernacles?

He taught in the Temple on the Feast of Tabernacles. Although His disciples had not expected Jesus to attend the feast, even though every male in Israel was required to do so, the vast majority of the pilgrims from afar who had heard of Him entertained the hope that they might see Him at Jerusalem. They were not disappointed, for Jesus did go to the Temple and on several occasions He taught in Solomon's Porch and elsewhere in the temple courts. These teachings were really the official or formal announcement of the divinity of Jesus to the Jewish people and to the whole world. Jesus risked His life to go to the Feast of Tabernacles, but the audacious boldness of Jesus in publicly appearing in Jerusalem overawed his enemies; they were not prepared for such a daring challenge.

On the last and greatest day of the Feast of Tabernacles (the day the Rabbis poured the water) Jesus stood (calling special attention to his message) and proclaimed Himself the very fountain of living water (John 7:37-38). On this last day of the Festival several special rituals and customs made the day more like a full festival day than any of the intermediate days. During the Water-drawing Celebration on this day, instead of circling the altar one time with the golden pitcher, the priest circled it seven times. Willows, cut from the riverbank and carried into the Temple by the priests were waved and then laid against the altar, forming a sukkot or canopy of drooping branches over the altar.

Isaiah 12:3 is quoted *"Therefore with joy shall ye draw water out of the wells of salvation."* Yeshua in Hebrew (Jesus in Greek) means "salvation." "Psalm 118:25 which reads, *"O Lord, save us"* is cried out by the people. Psalm 118 is viewed as a Messianic psalm and as such gave the feast a Messianic emphasis. This is why Jesus was greeted by the crowds shouting Hosanna (Hebrew for "Save now" in Ps. 118:25) and waving palm branches on His triumphal entry into Jerusalem (Mt. 21:8-9). They viewed Him as the Messiah King, come to deliver ('save now') Israel in fulfillment of Psalm 118. They hailed Him with the Messianic imagery of palm branches from the Feast of Tabernacles. This same imagery is in view in Rev. 7:9-10 where redeemed saints worship, with palm branches in hand, around the throne of God and the Lamb (9)."

It was in this context that Jesus spoke to the crowded worshippers in the Temple and declared that *"If anyone is thirsty, let him come to me and drink. Whoever believes in me, as the Scripture has said, streams of living water will flow from within him ."* (John 7:37-39) "In other words, He said: I am the answer to your prayers. I am the Messiah. I can save you now so that you will never thirst for salvation again (10)."

Later during the Feast Jesus stood and declared to His people *"I am the light of the world. Whoever follows me will never walk in darkness, but will have the light of life" (John 8:12)*. "The light from the Feast of Tabernacles lamps illuminated the whole city." (11). The light represented the Shekinah glory that once filled the temple where God's presence dwelt in the Holy of Holies. During this time, the Temple was thought of as the light of the world.

In the healing of the blind man, Jesus combined two very important themes of Tabernacles (John 9:1-12). He again stated that He was the light of the world (v. 5) and He emphasized water once more when He told the man to go wash in the pool of Siloam upon which he was healed (v. 7). All of Jerusalem's attention was on this pool during the Feast.

### *Some other ways in which Jesus fulfilled this feast are:*

**Jesus is the Living Water:** Our spiritual thirst cannot be quenched with anything less than Christ. *But whosoever drinketh of the water that I shall give him shall never thirst; but the water that I shall give him shall be in him a well of water springing up into everlasting life (John 4:14).*

**Jesus Washes Away Our Sins:** Jesus is the true living water cleansing us from sin through His blood. *For if the blood of bulls and of goats, and the ashes of an heifer sprinkling the unclean, sanctifieth to the purifying of the flesh: How much more shall the blood of Christ, who through the eternal Spirit offered himself without spot to God, purge your conscience from dead works to serve the living God (Heb. 9:13-14).*

**Jesus is the Light of the World:** The light from the Feast of Tabernacles lamps illuminated the whole city. Scholars suggest that Jesus referred to this custom when he spoke those well-known words, " *I am the light of the world…" (John 8:12 also see John 1:1-9 and John 9:5).*

**Jesus is Preparing Our Permanent Home:** These physical bodies we now occupy are only temporary dwelling places. Our bodies are frail, and will eventually begin to deteriorate. Life is short. Our hope is not in what the world has to offer, but in what God has already provided for us for eternity. Our permanent home is being prepared for us in eternity. Jesus said in John 14:2-3, *In my Father's house are many mansions: if it were not so, I would have told you. I go to prepare a place for you. And if I go and prepare a place for you, I will come again, and receive you unto myself; that where I am, there ye may be also.* Matthew Henry states: "…then He left his mansions of light above to tabernacle among us (John 1:14), and He dwelt in booths. And the worship of God under the New Testament is prophesied of under the notion of keeping the feast of tabernacles, (Zec. 14:16). For, the gospel of Christ teaches us to dwell in tabernacles, to sit loose to this world, as those that have here no continuing city, but by faith, and hope and holy contempt of present things, to go out to Christ without the camp (Heb. 13:13, 14).

One interesting side note is that the early church believed that Jesus was born on the Feast of Tabernacles. Scholars cite several evidences for this belief:

1. The shepherds were in the fields with their flock when Jesus was born. The Talmud – Mas. Ta'anith 2a Chapter 2 states that the rainy season began at the time of the Feast of Tabernacles. This has a great deal to do with the reasons for the activities and prayers connected to the last day - the Great Day – of the Feast. Thus the flocks around Bethlehem were normally brought in from the fields and sheltered until spring. So the sheep would not have been in the fields in December.

2. When the angels announced Jesus' birth to the startled shepherds, they used Feast of Tabernacles terminology. Luke 2:10 "Do not be afraid. I bring you good news of great joy that will be for all the people."
>
> a. Tabernacles is called "the season of our joy"--"good news of great joy"
>
> b. Tabernacles is called "the feast of the nations" --"for all the people."

3. We can date Jesus' conception from Elizabeth's pregnancy with John the Baptist. Zechariah was serving in the Temple when God told him he would father a son.

a) Temple service was divided up between the priests so that each priest was scheduled to serve for two non-consecutive weeks in addition to all of the divisions of priests serving during the three pilgrimage feasts. Zechariah was a part of the 8th division of priests and thus would minister in the temple during the 10th week of the year. (The weeks of Passover and Pentecost would not be counted because all of the priests were required to be in Jerusalem for them).

b) By this calculation, John the Baptist would have been born during Passover. It is interesting to note that the angel of God told Zechariah that his son would possess "the spirit and power of Elijah". Remember that a place is set at the Passover Seder for Elijah because of Scripture that indicate that Elijah will be a fore-runner of the Messiah.

c. Elizabeth was six month pregnant when the angel Gabriel appeared to Mary. This would have been around the 25th of Kislev, or on Chanukah. Jesus may have been conceived during the festival of Chanukah and that would put His birth during the Feast of Tabernacles.

4. Because this was a pilgrimage feast, Jerusalem was crowded. The Romans would often declare tax time during a Temple feast due to the difficulties with travel. The term "sukkot" can be translated "stable" so Jesus may have been born in a booth (see Gen. 33:17).

5. The Apostle John, in describing the birth of Jesus, used Tabernacles terminology. John 1:14 "The Word became flesh and made his dwelling among us."

6. Eight days after His birth, Jesus was circumcised into the Abrahamic covenant according to Luke 2:21. If Jesus were born on the first day of the feast, His circumcision would correspond to the festival Shemini Atzeret which is the eighth day of the Feast of Tabernacles also called "The Great Day".

### *Conclusion*

In summary, the Feast of Tabernacles was a joyful commemoration of the divine guidance granted to the Atonement, the idea of joy after redemption was naturally very prominent. In a decreased daily scale a special sacrifice of seventy bullocks was made. The temple-trumpets were blown on each day. There was the ceremony of the outpouring of water, drawn from Siloam, in memory of the refreshing stream, which had come miraculously out of the rock at Meribah (Ex. 17:1-7), and in anticipation of blessings both for Israel and for the world. There was the illumination of the inner court of the temple, where the light of the grand candelabra reminded one of the pillar of fire by night which had served as a guide through the desert (Num. 14:14). There was a torch-parade. And above all, everywhere in and around Jerusalem, in the street, the square, and even on the roofs of the houses booths were erected. These leafy dwellings provided shelter for the pilgrims who came from every direction to attend this feast. But most of all they too were reminders of the exodus wilderness-life of the ancestors (Lev. 23:43) (12).

This holiday reminds us not to hold too tightly to material things. We live in a very materialistic age. When the Israelites were wanderers in the desert, they all lived in tents–rich and poor alike. Material possessions can control and manipulate us; they become gods, or idols, over us. We must remember that this life is only temporary. We are also on a pilgrimage to a Promised Land in eternity. We need to seek God's kingdom, not earthly comfort. As we seek first the Kingdom of God (Luke 12:31), God is our shelter. *For thou hast been a strength to the poor, a strength to the needy in his distress, a refuge from the storm, a shadow from the heat, when the blast of the terrible ones is as a storm against the wall (Isa. 25:4).*

This Feast teaches us that our lives and hearts should be filled to overflowing with thanksgiving to God for how He has delivered us from sin and death and hell. How we need to praise Him for giving us salvation and eternal life with Him and how we need to spend our lives in the joyous worship of our Savior just as we will also do throughout eternity. This is a holiday looking back at past blessings and deliverance, rejoicing in the present forgiveness of sins and salvation and looking forward to the day when we will be united with our Lord and Savior to live all eternity in His glory.

But there is also the responsibility to share this good news with the world. At this feast, Jesus stands publicly in the temple and declares Himself to be the "Living Water" and to be the "Light of the World". He is public, He is giving the message and He is calling the people to saving faith in Him. This feast is a day of rejoicing for all those who have been covered in the atonement, whose sins have been forgiven and they are one with the Heavenly Father. And we must take this good news to those who are still outside and "unatoned" for. Jesus says in Matthew 28, *"Then Jesus came to them and said, "All authority in heaven and on earth has been given to me. 19Therefore go and make disciples of all nations, baptizing them in the name of the Father and of the Son and of the Holy Spirit, 20and teaching them to obey everything I have commanded you. And surely I am with you always, to the very end of the age."*

And in Acts 1, *"It is not for you to know the times or dates the Father has set by his own authority. 8But you will receive power when the Holy Spirit comes on you; and you will be my witnesses in Jerusalem, and in all Judea and Samaria, and to the ends of the earth."*

## Footnotes for Chapter Nine

1- Victor Buksbazen. *The Gospel in the Feasts of Israel* . p. 44.
2- Irving Greenberg. *The Jewish Way* . p. 26.
3- Ibid.
4- David W. Brown. *Succoth: The Feast of Tabernacles* . AMF International.
5- Robert Boyd. *Exploring Israel's History* . p. 232
6- Alfred Edershiem. *The Temple* . p. 178.
7- Kevin Howard and Marvin Rosenthal. *The Feasts of the Lord* . p. 136.
8- Alfred Edershiem. *The Temple* . p. 187.
9- Kevin Howard and Marvin Rosenthal. *The Feasts of the Lord* . p. 196.
10- Ibid. p. 142.
11- Scarlata, Robin and Linda Pierce, *A Family Guide to the Biblical Holidays.* p. 352.
12- William Hendriksen, *Exposition of the Gospel According to John* , vol. 2, p. 4

### The Feast of Trumpets – Effectual Calling of the Holy Spirit
This feast is the beginning of a season of repentance culminating in the Day of Atonement. It emphasizes a desire to strive for atonement of our sins of the past year and longs for forgiveness and salvation by God's calling. The focus of forgiveness in this feast however, is on God's willingness to give us forgiveness out of his own goodness and love for us. " *Good and upright is the LORD; Therefore He instructs sinners in the way" (Psalm 25:8). "Return to Him from whom you have deeply defected, O sons of Israel" (Isaiah 31:6). "Return, O faithless sons, I will heal your faithlessness. Behold, we come to You For You are the LORD our God" (Jeremiah 3:22).* In this feast Israel was called to repent of their sin and make ready for the Day of Atonement.

### The Days of Awe – Confession and Repentance
For the Jews, these days are a mixture of works and grace, of repentance and forgiveness, of charity and synagogue attendance. They examine themselves to see if their good works and faithful obedience to the law have been enough to earn God's favor, forgiveness of sin and heaven. As Christians we are to also be examining ourselves and following the exhortation from I John 1:8 *8If we claim to be without sin, we deceive ourselves and the truth is not in us. 9If we confess our sins, he is faithful and just and will forgive us our sins and purify us from all unrighteousness. 10If we claim we have not sinned, we make him out to be a liar and his word has no place in our lives.* But they are also looking to the Day of Atonement and God's grace the day when they pray that a loving God will accept them and love them and forgive their sins.)

### Day of Atonement – Justification
God presented Jesus as a sacrifice of atonement, and the means of justification through faith in His blood. Jesus' death surpasses and replaces the atonement ritual of the Jewish Temple. The book of Hebrews explains the ceremonies of the Day of Atonement as a pattern of the atoning work of Christ. Jesus is our high priest, and His blood shed on Calvary is seen as being symbolized in the blood of bulls and goats. No other sacrifice would ever be needed again before the Heavenly Father for our salvation nor would any other sacrifice ever again be accepted. Jesus had done the permanent and final work of salvation on the cross. Everything that is needed has been done and by God's righteous decree the blood of Jesus is applied to the hearts of all those who believe in Christ alone.

### The Feast of Tabernacles - Perseverance of the Saints
This feast reminds us that we have the responsibility to share this good news with the world. At this feast Jesus stands publicly in the temple and declares

Himself to be the "Living Water" and to be the "Light of the World". He is public, He is giving the message and He is calling the people to saving faith in Him. This feast is a day of rejoicing for all those who have been covered in the atonement, whose sins have been forgiven and they are one with the Heavenly Father. And we must take this good news to those who are still outside and "unatoned" for. Jesus says in Matthew 28 " *18Then Jesus came to them and said, "All authority in heaven and on earth has been given to me. 19Therefore go and make disciples of all nations, baptizing them in the name of the Father and of the Son and of the Holy Spirit, 20and teaching them to obey everything I have commanded you. And surely I am with you always, to the very end of the age."* And in Acts 1 *"It is not for you to know the times or dates the Father has set by his own authority. 8But you will receive power when the Holy Spirit comes on you; and you will be my witnesses in Jerusalem, and in all Judea and Samaria, and to the ends of the earth."* The Lord expects us to be making disciples until He returns.

# Bibliography

*S.Y. Agnon. Days of Awe* . New York, New York, Schocken Books, 1975 – 295 pages. A Teasury of Jewish Wisdom for Reflection, Repentance and Renewal on the High Holy Days.

Samuel Bacchiocchi. *God's Festivals in Scripture and History, Part 1 – The Spring Festivals.* Berrien Springs, Michigan, Biblical Perspectives, 1995 – 252 pages. This book is an attempt to show how the festivals of God benefit the church today.

J. Sidlow Baxter. *Explore the Book.* Grand Rapids, Michigan, 1966. A basic and broadly interpretive course of Bible study from Genesis to revelation.

Robert Boyd. *Exploring Israel's History.* Iowa Falls, IA., Word Bible Publishers, Inc., 2001 – 244 pages. This book recounts the past of Israel, explains it's present significance and anticipates in future in God's plan for His people and His coming Kingdom.

Victor Buksbazen. *The Gospel in the Feasts of Israel.* Philadelphia, PA, The Friends of Israel Missionary and Relief society, Inc., 1955 – 80 Pages. An explanation of the customs and practices, as well as the beliefs of the Jewish people.

Alfred Edershiem. *The Temple.* Grand Rapids, Michigan, Kregal Publications, 1874 – 256 Pages. This book is about the Temple, its ministry and its services as they were in the time of Christ on earth.

Alfred Edershiem. *Sketches of Jewish Social Life.* Peabody, MA., Hendrickson Publishers, 1994 – 307 pages. This is the classical study of the cultural and social world of Jesus and His apostles.

Mitch and Zhava Glaser. *The Fall Feasts of Israel.* Chicago, IL, Moody Press, 1987 - 256 Pages. Understanding the purpose and traditions of the Jewish feasts will give you a deeper appreciation for your God, your heritage, and the gift of redemption provided by the sacrificial death of Christ.

Louis Goldberg. *Our Jewish Friends.* Neptune, NJ, Loizeaux Brothers, 1977 – 188 Pages. Dr. Goldberg clearly describes Jewish holidays, religious practices and doctrines. He gives valuable suggestions to the Christian desiring to lead a Jewish person to the Messiah.

Joseph Good. *Rosh Hashanah and the Messianic Kingdom to Come*. Port Arthur, TX. Hatikva Ministries, 1989 – 197 pages. A Messianic Jewish Interpretation of the Feasts of Trumpets.

Philip Goodman. *The Rosh Hashanah Anthology*. Jerusalem, Israel, The Jewish Publication Society, 1970 – 379 Pages. This anthology is intended to make meaningful the religious impact and the manner of commemoration of the Jewish New Year both as a solemn day and as a festive day.

Philip Goodman. *The Shauvot Anthology*. Philadelphia, PA., The Jewish Publication Society of America, 1974 – 369 Pages. This anthology aims to convey the spirit of the festival in its many diverse aspects.

Michael Grant. *The Jews in the Roman World*. New York, New York, Barnes and Noble Books, 1973 – 330 pages. This book shows us the period of history in which the Jewish religion virtually assumed it's final form.

Irving Greenberg. *The Jewish Way*. New York, New York, Summit Books, 1988 – 448 pages. This is a comprehensive and compelling presentation of Judaism as revealed through it's holy days.

Kevin Howard and Marvin Rosenthal. *The Feasts of the Lord*. Nashville, TN. Thomas Nelson Inc., 1997 – 224 pages. This book covers all aspects of the biblical feasts – historical background, biblical observance, modern observance, and prophetic significance.

Marguerite Ickis. *The Book of Religious Holidays and Celebrations*. New York, New York, Dodd, Mead & Company, 1966 – 161 Pages. This book describes the religious holidays and celebrations that serve to unite churches and give continuity to religious thought and purpose from the rich traditions of the Jewish and Christian faiths.

Joan R. Lipis. *Celebrate Passover Haggadah*. San Francisco, CA., Purple Pomegranate Productions, 1996 – 56 Pages. A Christian presentation of the Traditional Jewish Festival.

Ernest L. Martin. *The Temples that Jerusalem Forgot*. Portland, OR., ASK Publications, 2000 – 485 pages. This is a study of the archaeological developments concerning the Temples of Israel and the Temple Mount and our understanding of them Scripturally and Spiritually.

Nosson Scherman, Hersh Goldwurm and Avie Gold. *Rosh Hashanah – Its Significance, Laws and Prayers*. Brooklyn, NY, Mesorah Publications, Ltd.,

1983 – 126 pages. The essence of Rosh Hashanah is presented in the language and perspective of today's intellectually curious Jew.

Michael Strassfeld. *The Jewish Holidays, A Guide & Commentary*. New York, New York, Harper & Row Publishers, 1985 – 248 Pages. This book will help us to understand more fully the meaning of the Jewish holidays and thereby to observe these festivals with greater devotion and joy.

Joseph Tulushkin. *Jewish Literacy*. New York, New York. William Morrow and Company, Inc., 1991 – 688 Pages. This is a compilation of the most important things to know about the Jewish religion, its people and its history.

William Whiston. *The Works of Flavius Josephus*. Grand Rapids, Michigan, Associated Publishers and Authors, Inc. This work is regarded as the only reference in history containing valid contemporary references to Christ. This book offers detailed accounts of Jewish life in the first century.

Made in the USA
Middletown, DE
05 April 2023

28306663R00066